"How C

Activating

Your Life"

A Memoir by:

Dr. Tina Omorogbe

KING JESUS PRESS LLC

DEDICATION

You, O Lord, deserve all the praise, glory, and honor for the wonderful works you have done in my life. It is with great humility that I give thanks to my heavenly Father, Jesus Christ my savior, and the Holy Spirit - my very best friend. I dedicate this book to my mother who passed on to meet the LORD on September 9, 2021. She was my best friend and my hero. My mother was an exceptional, dedicated, loving and compassionate mother and wife. Mother was a great woman of God, a prayer warrior, a lover of God, and a lover of people! She was a phenomenal woman, kind, honest, humble, selfless and beautiful. You are greatly missed, Mom. Rest on, until we meet again.

In honor of my mother, 50 percent of the proceeds from this book will finance start-up fees for small businesses for women in Nigeria who are struggling to keep their small business afloat and for those who lack the finance to start a small business to support their children and families.

CONTENTS

FOREWORD

Shortly after acknowledging my call to preach the Gospel in 2007, God spoke to me audibly and told me, "Angela, if you are to reach the hearts of the people, you must be transparent when you stand before them." I wish I could tell you that the encounter was enough for me to move forward in my calling; however, it was not, and I did not immediately heed God's voice. Like Jacob, I wrestled with God about this, and I did not share my testimony. I sheltered my witness, and as a result, my confidence in my calling was likened to 'imposter syndrome." I knew without a doubt that I had been called to preach the Gospel, but I could not understand why God would call me, yet not allow me to flourish in my calling.

For several years following that conversation, I continued to wrestle with God until one day, I lamented and cried out to Him with this question. "Lord, why do I need to be this transparent? Nobody cares about my story." And immediately, once again, God spoke to me (audibly) and said, "I care. You tell your story so that they can be healed." It was out of those conversations with God that it became very clear to me that my ministry would be authentic, transparent, and touch people's hearts so that healing would take place in the body of Christ.

I met Dr. Tina Omorogbe over 10 years ago, and immediately, our spirits connected. However, it was not until two years ago, when Tina invited me to her home after Sunday church service to talk and have tea, that our spiritual bond was created. We laughed, cried, praised God, and shared our love for Christ.

During that gathering, we shared some of our personal encounters with God and our mutual desires to be constantly in God's presence. What was most memorable about our afternoon delight was that Tina spoke unapologetically about her audible conversations with God, which is a rarity in the body of Christ.

Dr. Omorogobe is vulnerable in this writing. It has been my experience that although many Christians want that type of connection with God, most do not dare to seek out or even disclose these encounters for fear of being misunderstood.

As I read Tina's memoir, two Scriptures immediately appeared. The first Scripture is, "*As the deer pants for the water, so my soul pants for You, O God. My soul thirsts for the living God.*" This writing is a brook of water for a soul that is thirsty for His presence, His power, and His will to be released in your life. This writing is significant, practical, and beneficial to Christ's body, especially for you, should you desire to drink from His brook of living water.

I cried and praised God as I read Chapter Two, "Trust Matters." It is a treasure trove that will bless you with precious, authentic insight into the various ways in which we should trust God.

Dr. Omorogbe shares her personal encounters and conversations with God and encourages you with practical guidance in chapter 6 (Hearing From God) to attune your ear to hear God's voice via various methods, including one I particularly embraced, which she refers to as "Impressions in Your Heart."

The second Scripture is, "*And they overcame him by the blood of the Lamb and by the word of their testimony and they loved not their lives unto death.*" (KJV) Tina's witnessing of Satan's attempts to quiet her and postpone the life God had in store for her has made her victorious through Christ. It has helped others experience God's saving power in their healing and faith, and she shares this with you in this work.

In this book, Tina recalls the many ways in which God's presence and power were a constant in her life and imparts with you what

I like to refer to as her *"God moments"* and shares with you her humor, and her walk of faith with obedience, joy, pain, grief, sorrow, evangelism, and her undeniable faith, trust and Love of God so that you can develop your own personal relationship and experience encounters with God that will unleash and activate His presence and power in your life.

This book is inspiring and touches the spirit. I encourage you to read it with an open heart and a listening ear to hear what the Lord says!

Rev. Dr. Angela West
Associate Minister, Union Missionary Baptist Church, Albany, NY

INTRODUCTION

Growing up, I had no big dreams for myself. For me, life was simple. I would become a nurse, get married, have kids, and serve God until He calls me home. Although my dreams seemed straightforward, I had no plans on how to achieve them. I allowed life to happen to me. And that meant most of the time I went wherever the wind of life took me. So, for many years, I went through the roller coaster of life. Can you relate to this?

There have been many personal challenges, struggles, emotional scars, and, of course, some blessings along the way. Looking back, I see that God, through His grace, perfectly tailored my life experiences and encounters to His perfect will for me regardless whether the experiences were good or bad. Through it all, God was always present in my circumstances, even when I did not feel or recognize His presence.

Becoming an author was the last thing I ever thought I would do. Even as I wrote this book, I constantly asked myself, "What do you think you are doing? Who is going to read *your* book? Why on earth do you think anyone wants to hear your story?" But an opposing, more gentle voice would tell me I am supposed to tell my story, and someone is waiting to hear it.

For more than a decade, I struggled as the Holy Spirit worked to reveal my potential. He would constantly tell me to take a leap of faith and to trust Him. The dreams and revelations I have encountered are nothing close to what I ever imagined for myself. It reminds me of *Jeremiah 29:11 (NIV), "For I know the plans I have for you," declares the LORD, "plans to prosper you and not to harm you, plans to give you hope and a future."* I was minding my own business one day, when I heard the Lord say, "I want you to tell your story." Little did I know the mandate would turn into a book. I cannot express the trepidation that gripped my heart when the thought of writing came to my mind. I had no fear of telling someone my story face-to-face, but the thought of articulating my journey to an audience of readers terrified me, largely because English is not my first language.

Even with my hesitancy to tell my story, I knew I could not keep my experiences to myself. In this memoir, "How Can I Forget," I expound on God's unconditional love and how He showed up in my life through my adversities and brokenness. In Chapter 1, I share personal and intimate stories to help you, the reader, understand how God's love can extend to you, too, and how the Holy Spirit can help you understand the depth of God's love.

Chapter 2 highlights the definition of trust and the security it brings once we trust God with everything. To help illustrate this point, I break this chapter into several subheadings to dissect various aspects of trust: vulnerable trust, complete trust, obedient trust, peaceful trust, promising trust, confident trust, and timely trust.

In Chapter 3, readers get a lesson on how to release the blessings from God through the power of forgiveness. Alternatively, when we do not forgive others as Jesus has instructed us, there are negative consequences. God had to really work on me in this area, as I am sure He has to work on a lot of you.

Most of us cannot live without our mobile phones. We use them daily, as they are multi-functional, and we would be lost without them. Once we drain the battery, we have to connect the phone to the charger because it is no longer functional. In Chapter 4, I outline the importance of staying connected to God. He is our power source, the charge that keeps us going.

My entire life is a walking testimony, and in Chapter 5 is a lesson on how to activate your own faith. My entire life is a walking testimony, and in this chapter you will learn about how I overcame many situations through faith. There is a lesson here for you on how to activate your own faith.

Every Christian wants to hear from God, but are you willing to be still long enough to actually hear Him? Chapter 6 lists all the various ways I have heard God speak to me throughout my walk with Him and guides you on how you can hear from Him too.

In the final chapter, the one that bears the name of the book, I reflect on all the marvelous works of God in my life. I have been able to accomplish so much through God's revelations – far greater than I could have imagined.

You are about to encounter the power, grace and mercies of God as you read through this book. I hope my story will help you take the first step to *your* greatness.

Chapter 1

MY LOVE JOURNEY

For many years, I thought I understood the meaning of love until I encountered some life challenges that needed to be conquered by love. Love is a powerful word, although most of the time we use the word casually without being conscious of what it really means. I believe, if we are intentional about love, our relationships with God, family and friends will be fruitful and more pleasurable. When we embrace love, we are equipped to handle some of the most difficult challenges in life. Love is something we all have to learn and adapt to, because ideally, it is going to cost us something to love. Love is not a straightforward path. It can be complex and complicated at times.

So, what is love? One of the Merriam-Webster Dictionary definitions of love is *"A strong affection for another arising out of kinship or personal ties, or attraction based on sexual desire; affection and tenderness felt by lovers."* It is caring and giving to someone else in a selfless way. I believe our love expressions and emotions are partly influenced by our cultural upbringing. When we deal with people from all walks of life daily, learning to love within diverse cultures can be complicated at times. It is not a simple task to carry out. It takes wisdom and understanding to build a loving relationship.

No one apart from God and yourself can really measure your love for another person, because love is an emotion that comes from your innermost being. We all know our hearts! Our actions and behavior toward a person can sometimes portray how we care for that person. Each of us appreciates love languages differently. As a result, it becomes tough at times to identify when genuine love is expressed by others. One of the problems is that when we say, "I love you," we do not exactly explain why we say we love someone. Generally, no one explains why they say they love a person except if the receiver asks why. The person receiving the love message may have their own reason why they felt they were loved. That said, if the receiver finds out that the reason they got a love message was different from what they thought, it may sometimes create a hard feeling or misunderstanding in a relationship causing unnecessary pains and arguments. Every one of us wants to be loved the way we want to be loved. Frankly, love is bigger than us, and we need a lot of help and training to communicate it correctly.

There are four types of love: *eros, philia, storge and agape* love. The Merriam-Webster Dictionary describes eros love as physical love or sexual desire. It is considered intimate and passionate. I feel this type of love is mostly based on physical attraction, which can be superficial. During courtship, the relationship is exciting and sweet because each person gets their initial love needs met. But as the relationship grows and demands more sacrificial love, sometimes people tend to pull away because once their immediate needs have been met, they realize they are not ready to make a sacrificial commitment. One reason why some relationships end up in bitterness and pain is because they were based on sexual gratification. Eros love has a very short shelf life, just like sex does. There is a problem when people who are madly in love end with confusion, despair and loneliness. We see many eros marriages and relationships today. In this type of relationship, it is important to know early on during courtship why your partner wants to be with you so you are not disillusioned. There are countless assumptions of what love is in the minds of many individuals. When people say they love you, we must go deeper to find out why. Love is not something we put on and take off when we want to. Love should be what defines us as a person. Love is infinite. Sadly, we cannot command people to love us because it is impossible to do so. Love comes from within, and we cannot give what we do not have.

The Merriam-Webster Dictionary describes philia love as a friendship feeling toward another person. This is generally with mutual friends. It is a relationship that holds some emotional strong bond that appeals to both parties. It is these common shared values and interests that keep the relationship going and strong. Every now and then you will find a friend whose friendship and love are greater than that of a close family member.

The Collins Online English Dictionary defines storge love as natural or instinctual affection, as of a parent for a child. It is a motherly type of love. An innate love that just flows out of a mother to a child, so much that you cannot help yourself even if the child does not meet your expectations. It is a genuine love. As parents, when our children offend us, we always find it in our heart to forgive them and love them through their weaknesses. No matter how bad they may seem, our love for them never dies. For some parents that love may be buried, perhaps, due to past hurts, hate or betrayals, but their love for their children never expires.

The Merriam-Webster Dictionary describes agape love as brotherly love. The Holy Bible speaks a lot about agape love as a sacrificial type of love. The kind of love God gave us when he gave His only begotten son Jesus Christ to die for the sins of the entire human race. *John 3:16 (NIV) says, "For God so loved the word that he gave his one and only Son, that whosoever believes in him shall not perish but have eternal life."* It is a love that is given without asking for favors in return. It is a selfless love and it crosses all boundaries. Meaning, no matter how messed up we are, God's love crosses over to meet us just as we are and where we are. It is calming, peaceful, gratifying and it lasts forever because it never fails. How can that be, you asked? Because God is love. That is who He is! Everything He does, is wrapped in love.

Although there are many types of love as I have mentioned, agape love is the one that has directed my love journey. I have lived long enough to truly say that the love the world offers is short-lived. It can sometimes be disappointing and can leave a bad taste in your mouth. Agape love is not a reciprocated love, but a sacrificial love. It requires you to surrender all that you are and have to the one you love. Such love brings you joy, peace and happiness. A non-reciprocated love can sometimes lead to a feeling of depression, loneliness, frustration, pain and hurt. I have come to realize that God's love is not for special people. It is for all people, and it does not discriminate. No one is excluded except those who exclude themselves. God's love does not bring condemnation, but rather, it brings correction. *Proverbs 3:11 (NIV) says, "My son, do not despise the Lord's discipline, and do not resent his rebuke."* Trust me, no one can measure God's love. It is too high for you to see, it is too wide for you to wrap your hands or thoughts around, and it is too deep for you to comprehend.

My experience with God's love is only the tip of the iceberg. Throughout my lifetime, I have come to understand quite a bit about His love. Thanks to the help of the Holy Spirit who is my helper, my director, and the one who leads me to all truth. *Job 14:1 (NKJV) says, "Man who is born of a woman is of few days and full of trouble."* As humans, we are bound to go through trials and tribulations of which I had my own share. There was a season in my life when I went through some difficult life challenges. During that season, I had no one to turn to but God. Nevertheless, it was not easy to turn to God until He closed every other avenue of help and communication, which forced me to turn to Him and communicate with Him face-to-face. Afterall, that was what God created us to do, to commune with Him.

During that season, I knew I was done trying to handle situations on my own. I had to surrender my life completely to God. As we grow in God, He allows us to go through trials in our lives that will rock our boat to bring us to our knees, allowing us to realize we did not create ourselves. He allows the enemy an opportunity to try us, but never to take our lives. This happened to a man of integrity in the Bible named Job, who feared God and stayed away from evil. During my difficult season, it seemed like God had abandoned me. It felt like He was nowhere close, and I felt like I was going to die. I felt lonely, helpless and hopeless, and the season seemed like it would never come to an end. But, what I did not know then was that it was not only a learning season in my life, but a process that would prepare me for God's divine purpose for my life. I knew it was time to take God seriously and to stay focused on Him. It was through this journey that I placed my thoughts and whole being under the leadership of the Holy Spirit. I believe the best place for us to encounter God's power and glory is through our adversities and brokenness.

My previous storms remind me of a story I once heard about a goldsmith who, during the process of purifying gold, sat by the fiery furnace and placed the non-purified gold into it. He kept his eyes on it because too much heat could destroy the gold. The goldsmith knew the amount of heat appropriate to purify the gold and the right timing to remove it from the furnace. The question is, can we trust God enough with our lives to purify us? Isaiah 48:10 (NKJV) s*ays, "Behold, I have refined you, but not as silver; I have tested you in the furnace of affliction."* 1 Corinthians 10:13 (NKJV) says, *"No temptation has overtaken you except such as is common to man; but God is faithful, who will not allow you to be tempted beyond what you are able, but with the temptation will also make the way of escape, that you may be able to bear it."*

So, whatever you are going through, God knows how much heat you can bear and how much time in that heat is needed to purify you. Most of all, He knows that you are coming out of the furnace golden! How much purification are you willing to allow God to do in your life? Your purification will determine your attraction, your price, and your influence. I had to go through this purification process. It was not about the other people in my life. God was concerned about me. It was me who needed cleansing and purifying. It was not an easy journey. It was a slow, painful and long process that eventually gave birth to greater things in my life. The Holy Spirit can transform your life if you allow Him to purify you like He did in my life.

I urge you to allow God to purify you today. He will teach you how to embrace your pain with His grace and love as He begins to work in your heart, mind and soul. With time, I slowly came out of my pains and struggles, and I believe you, too, will come out of yours as you allow God to use your trials and tribulations to draw you closer to Him and heal you. I watched God work on my behalf as I rested my head on His shoulder.

No matter what you are going through, God's eyes are on you. Even if you feel like God has abandoned you, He has not; He is only trying to purify you, and when He does, the world will admire His handy work and see you as an overcomer. You are one of the stars in the sky. People will be drawn to you. Glory to God!

It is through this journey of my life that God began to teach me what it really means to love. I learned that pure love has no desire to be reciprocated. You know what I mean? You rub my back, and I'll rub yours. Many of us practice love this way. But this type of attitude does not portray true love. It is true that many of us have gone a distance to show our loved ones and friends how much we love them. However, when there is no sign of affirmation and appreciation of our love to them, we often become resentful, hurtful and bitter. So, be mindful not to occupy yourselves with these mind games. By all means, live freely and love freely.

I learned from my experiences that God's love is always present to guide and protect us, not because of who we are or what we have done. Matthew 5:45b (NKJV) says, *"He causes his sun to rise on the evil and the good, and sends rain on the righteous and the unrighteous."* Indeed, there is no limitation to God's love. His love crosses all boundaries. As I began to learn about God's love, I was humbled by his instructions and teachings. I started praying to God to bathe me with His love. Have you ever prayed to God for something, and He sends you a test to check your character and obedience? One time, I was in a heated and a crucial conversation with a loved one, and suddenly I heard this gentle voice say to me, do not be offended. At first, I was surprised the LORD would be interested in my conversation, then I realized I had given Him permission to be the master of my life. He was trying to save me from unnecessary conversations that would bring me distress and pain. Suddenly, this thought came to my mind that I, too, have offended others. I immediately deflated like a balloon, and I became less reactive and more humbled. After all, we are all broken people, and we need the savior, Jesus Christ. Frankly, there are also many times when I disobeyed the gentle sweet voice and acted out my way to please my flesh. And I also knew how the conversations ended. They were not pretty. I am grateful for the mercies of God in my life. I thank God for loving and correcting me. Proverbs 3:12 (NKJV) says, *"For whom the Lord loves He corrects, just as a father the son in whom he delights."* Are you ready to accept God's correction?

I was driving to work one morning and felt down. My heart was pretty heavy as I thought about how much love I had poured out on loved ones and how my love had been rejected and not appreciated. Tears began to run down my cheeks and I found myself asking God, "Why is it that my love has caused me so much pain?" At that moment, I heard Him say, *"It is love that kept Jesus on the cross."* It was like a wake-up call for me. Suddenly, I broke down and began to sob uncontrollably. My makeup and mascara were all over my face, and by the time I got to work, I was a basket case. This life changing experience reminded me about the true love of God to all mankind when He gave His only Son as a sacrificial offering on the cross for everyone. He took our place of death upon Himself so we could be reconciled with our heavenly Father and be free from condemnation and God's punishment. Through this act, He showed us how much He loved us. What an awesome and marvelous God we have for Him to lay His life down for a sinner like you and me! I was truly humbled. Here I was talking about the pain I felt of not being loved. But God was like, *I gave you all my love too! Did you really appreciate me and show me love for doing that?*

Some of us have lost it. We do not fear or respect God. What will it take for you to know God is the master of your life? We say and do whatever we want and do not care about how it makes God feel. Yet, God continues to show us His love and never gives up on us. God loves us so much, and He is in constant pursuit of us. A few years ago, I had an experience that impacted my life for good. A colleague of mine had a baby, and I went to the store to purchase a nice gift. I wrapped it with a beautiful gift wrap and put a nice blue bow on it. I was so excited and looked forward to seeing the joy on my colleague's face when she opened the gift. I called her several times to pick up the baby's gift, but she never showed up. I took it upon myself to deliver the gift to her at her place of work, but she was not there and no one would receive the gift on her behalf. Two weeks passed, and she still had not picked up the gift. I called her one more time, and she promised to pick it up but never showed up.

As I walked back to my office later that day with the gift in my hand, suddenly an overwhelming sadness enveloped me, and I began to speak to ask God why is it that I am running around trying to give a gift I bought with my money to someone who does not care about my gift? Suddenly, the Lord responded and said, *"This is how I feel when I am running after my children to give them my love and the gift of life, and they turn me down."* I was completely done. I began to cry! I cried so hard, I became numb and speechless. I was sincerely humbled by this experience. Immediately, I repented for all the times I was stubborn and disobedient to God. For all the times I gave deaf ears to His requests. I repented for the times I made God feel the way I felt that very day because I could relate, and it was not a great feeling. I will never forget that day in my life. Today, I am more sensitive and mindful about God's feelings in whatever I do.

When we obey God, it makes Him happy. Turning your back on Him makes Him very sad. Till this very day, my colleague never came to pick up the gift and I ended up giving it to someone else who was happy to receive it. Some of us are like my colleague in this story. God tries to give you the gift of life which He paid for by His gruesome death on the cross. But what do we do? We reject Him and turn our backs on Him. How would you feel if you went out of your way to buy a present for a friend or family member and they rejected the gift? It is never a good feeling. I want you to know the Lord is looking for people who are willing to receive His love. Will you accept His gift of love? Jesus

Christ is waiting at the door of your heart. Will you let Him in? I pray you receive him today and you will never regret it.

It is our responsibility to submit ourselves to God so He can use us for His glory. Jesus is the lover of our souls. He will continually come after us. Matthew 18:12 (NKJV) says, "*What do you think? If a man has a hundred sheep, and one of them goes astray, does he not leave the ninety-nine and go to the mountains to seek the one that is straying?* This is the kind of love Jesus is offering you and me. When He finds you, will you come with Him, or will you turn your back on Him?

We are all guilty of not loving! Jesus gave us two important commandments to guide us in the matter of love. *Matthew 22: 37-39 (NKJV) says, "You shall love the Lord your God with all your heart, with all your soul and with all your mind. This is the first and great commandment. And the second is like it: You shall love your neighbor as yourself."* The instructions are clear. It is important that we first love God with everything that is within us. Submit everything to Him. We must bring ourselves and our thoughts under His authority for our own good. We are instructed to love our neighbors as we love ourselves. But truth be told, some of us do not even love ourselves. How then can we love the people around us?

In my Christian journey, the first thing God taught me was to define who I was. During this process, I found out my weakness, my strengths, the things that threaten my faith, and my opportunities. After identifying these areas, I started working on my weaknesses. I learned about the characters of God. What does He like and dislike? As a result, I became more aware of my behavior and character.

I posted the values of a prudent woman written in Proverbs 31 at my workstation to remind me of what I should be like. This was helpful in my development to become a woman after God's own heart. I had to die to my flesh and my will by letting things like anger, bitterness, offensive spirit, and unforgiveness go.

One of my greatest strengths was my faith in the LORD. As I grew stronger in the LORD, I was willing to let go because of my love for God and His love for me. I was open to new opportunities to grow in the LORD by accepting invitations to speak about God on many platforms and holding yearly healing conferences for several years. Then, I started working on things that threatened my walk with the Lord. I took hold of the fears that held me bound. As God continued to share how much he loved me, I shut down the voices that said I was not good enough to talk about God or receive His love and kindness. I realized these voices were all a lie from the pit of hell. I am glad today that I overcame fear by the blood of the Lamb (Jesus Christ). You, too, can begin your journey by first evaluating your life and identifying what you need to work on. It is your responsibility to do so, and not your mother, father, spouse or pastor.

After you realize you are a sinner and not as good as you thought, turn your heart to Jesus, your Savior and Redeemer. He will then begin to mold and reshape your life so you can become more like Him and love like Him.

The second commandment is to love your neighbor as you love yourself. This is a huge challenge for many of us today. Loving your neighbor as you love yourself warrants you to first love yourself. Why would the LORD ask us to first love ourselves? Because he knows we cannot give what we do not have. We cannot draw water from a dry well or a pot. So, on my journey to love, I began to spend time with myself. I took time to care for myself and did things that made me happy. It was so refreshing and fulfilling to see my awesome Heavenly Father become the potter of my life.

Psalm 139:13 (NIV) says, *"For you created my inmost being; you knit me together in my mother's womb."* His love for me became my shield and my fortress. He protected me during all the opposition I faced. Slowly, God began to conquer my obstacles one at a time. But it was not an easy journey. I trusted God because God can be trusted. I did a lot of talking with Him, and He spoke to me. It was and continues to be a true relationship.

When you look at yourself in a mirror, what do you see? Well, you may say, I see my physical appearance. Ok, but what do you see when you look inward? The inner you is what defines you. It is important to take an inventory of what your inner self looks like. Some of us have experienced extreme trauma, assault of many types, and pains. These experiences have damaged the inner self of so many of us, and we are like dead among the living, a ticking time bomb, disconnected individuals, and filled with brokenness.

What do you say to yourself? Have you ever been around people who are always saying negative words about themselves? They say things like, "I am so stupid." "Nothing good ever comes my way." "I am too fat." "I am too thin." "I am not knowledgeable enough to run that business." "I am not good enough." "My English is not good enough." One of the reasons why we deal with these experiences could be because we have allowed other people's words to damage us. We have embraced the negative comments for so long that they have molded our thoughts and behaviors in the wrong direction. Therefore, we become what we think. Remember, whatever goes through our hearts and minds flows through us and drives our daily activities. If your well is dirty, that is what you will draw from and give to others. But, if you are a spring of living waters, that is what you will draw from and give to your neighbors, spouses, families, and friends. If you have hatred, bitterness, and jealousy in your heart, that is what you have to offer to those around you. Likewise, if you have joy, peace, kindness and love in your heart, that is what would flow out of you to others. It is true that a fruit does not fall far from its tree. Unfortunately, we cannot command people to love us. It is impossible, because love comes from within. It is deeper than what you think or feel. It is not a superficial feeling. It is a gift of God.

There was a time in my life when all I saw was my brokenness, my imperfection, my weaknesses, and my failures. It is interesting how the human mind seems to always bring to your attention the negative issues of your life, but rarely presents to you your strengths, and opportunities. It took the grace of God and His constant affirmation to convince me that I am not what my situation says I am. I was indeed created for greatness and for good works. We are God's reflection because we are made in His image and likeness. I also learned to let God define me and not others. This was the first step in knowing who I was and to whom I belong. I found a lot of bitterness, discontent and unhappiness in my heart. I was resentful and did a lot of complaining too. Eventually, I began to use the word of God to set boundaries for myself. I trusted that God would make things work out for my good because I loved Him.

Throughout my journey, I saw God's handiwork in every situation of my life. Some encounters were strategically orchestrated by God to drive me to the right place at the right time. I had to constantly remind myself of who my Heavenly Father was and tell myself I am an overcomer by the blood of the Lamb. *John 14:15 says, "If you love Me, you will do as I command."* The Spirit of God directs us to truth and to the perfect will of God. If you follow the instructions of God, He will teach you how to relate with your neighbors, families, spouses, and friends. James 1:19 says, *"Everyone should be quick to listen, slow to speak, and slow to become angry."* It makes God sad when He sees His children entangled in bitterness, hate and unforgiveness. Ecclesiastes 7:9 says, *"Do not be quick to anger, for anger lodges in the bosom of fools."* This Scripture helped me deal with my own anger issues. I thank God today that anger no longer dwells within me; it is a thing of the past. You, too, can begin your love journey by allowing the Spirit of God to take control of your life as He did for me.

It costs a lot to love. True love is a sacrificial love. The death of Jesus Christ exemplifies this type of love. Jesus took the gruesome beating and disgraceful insults from people who were not up to His level or standard. He tolerated so much pain and foolishness from many; He continues to do the same with us today. He carried my death, my suffering, my pains, and my shame. In John 19:30, Jesus says, *"...It is finished..."* at the cross. For as many who are ready to receive and embrace this gift, they shall live again and prosper on earth. My heart is full of joy and gratitude to the only one true God. I am forever grateful and thankful for all my life struggles and challenges, for He has made something beautiful out of my life. We must trust God when He is cutting, shaping and molding us after his own image and likeness. Just rest on God, and trust His process.

1 Corinthians 13:4-8 says, *"Love is patient, love is kind, love is not envious or boastful or arrogant or rude. It does not insist on its own way; it is not irritable or resentful; it does not rejoice in wrongdoing; but rejoices in truth."* God's words always correct me. He does not condemn me. If you feel condemned as you read the contents of this book, I want to assure you that it is not God. God loves us so much; all he wants to do is correct you as He did for me. *Hebrews 12:6 says this is "because the Lord disciplines the one he loves, and he chastens everyone he accepts as his son."* If you are not being corrected by God, you may be in serious trouble. The last thing we need is for God to turn His back on us. Our God is long suffering, and it takes a lot of rebelliousness for Him to finally pull back. Think about it. How would it make you feel if you have a child whom you have tried numerous times to correct, and he repeatedly ignored or refused to yield to your corrections? However, it makes you feel may very

well be the way it makes God feel - disappointed and hurt that His love and discipline is rejected. I also understand some of us have developed a cold and callous heart; nothing may bother us. If this is you, you need Jesus to haul away this coldness and fill your heart with His liquid love. It is difficult to explain this type of love, but I invite you to come and experience God for yourselves, so you will never go back to where you were.

The truth is that if we do not love the people in our lives, we do not love God, period! 1 John 4:20 reads, *"If someone says, 'I love God,' but hates a fellow believer, that person is a liar; for if we don't love people we can see, how can we love God, whom we cannot see?"* When we do not love the people around us, we may not care if they die or perish. But, when we love, we take risks to save our loved ones. After all, true love crosses all boundaries and love always wins! *1 John 4:7-8 says, "Beloved let us love one another, for love is from God, and whoever loves has been born of God and knows God. Anyone who does not love does not know God, because God is love."* I realized that I, too, must learn to love the way God loves. Although some of us are difficult to love, if we ask God for grace to love, He will give it to us. This is not an easy task to carry out. It is a daily practice and process.

Many of us spend so much time trying to get a person to accept our love. I want to remind you of the saying that we can bring a horse to the river, but you cannot force it to drink from the river. If a person continuously rejects your love, please do not get stuck there. Move on, and share your love with other people who are hurting or neglected. Not everyone that encountered Jesus took His offer for salvation and accepted His love. Remember, Jesus did not get stuck with them, He moved on to reach other people with His love. This was the reason He left his own town because many would not believe Him or accept His love. But, He went on doing good and healing people who needed what He had to offer. You should not waste your time either. We live in a broken world. If you are filled with so much love, share it with the people who are hurting around you. Be God's representative and bring your smiles, hugs and comfort to those who are lonely and hurting. Every one of us has an intense desire to be loved and nurtured.

So many people feel like everything has to be about them. It is either their way or no way. Frankly, it is not about you, and it will never be about you. We must learn to begin to see others as God sees them. People often may treat others wrong because it is what they have offered. Surely, We cannot give what we do not have. It is important for us to address our problems or issues before they overtake us. Remember, we cannot wish our problems and issues away! It is not that easy. It is important to face our problems no matter how big, small or bad they may seem. The longer you wait, the more damage you can cause yourself and those close to you. As you can see, it is not always about you.

In the book of Genesis, *God created man, and He saw that man was lonely. Then He put the man to sleep, took one of his ribs and created a woman. Genesis 2:24 says, "For this reason a man leaves his father and mother and is united to his wife, and they become one flesh."* So, if a man hates his wife, he hates himself! A man who beats his wife hates himself. A man who abuses his wife in any form or fashion hates himself. Conversely, a man who protects and loves his wife, loves himself. It is that simple. No one has the right to mistreat any human being in any relationship. This is exactly why we need the sacrificial type of love. Loving someone is a choice we make. We can learn to love those we feel are unlovable, but they must also be willing to receive the love that is extended to them.

Love is a beautiful thing. It is strong and powerful, but it is not any of the following:

- Love is NOT abusive.
- Love is NOT manipulative.
- Love is NOT a transaction.
- Love is NOT a game.
- Love is NOT conditional.
- Love is NOT perfection.

- Love is NOT abrasive.
- Love is NOT harsh.
- Love is NOT paranoid.

So many people are in love with the wrong things. They are in love with their jobs, cars, houses, educational degrees, or themselves, and they forget others. We have misplaced love on perishable things, while some have made themselves their own idols. Some of us do not love ourselves enough to do the right thing. This attitude or behavior has led to so much pain, not only in our own lives, but also in the lives of those around us. Do you love yourself? This is a question we should all ask ourselves. Today, we hear a lot about self-love. Perhaps, this may be due to too many people investing their time and love in others without being appreciated. Their love may not have been accepted, leaving them feeling betrayed, neglected and rejected.

Self-love is about giving love to yourself first and believing your needs and thoughts also matter. Afterall, the Bible also commands us to love ourselves. *Ephesians 5:29 reads, "For no one ever hated his own flesh, but nourishes and cherishes it, just as Christ does the church."* Still, there are some people who hate themselves. How do you expect someone to love you when you do not even love yourself? You cannot ask people to give you something you cannot give yourself. Self-love is a good thing, but be careful not to start worshiping yourself. It becomes a huge problem if we worship ourselves and forget the One, we should worship. *Matthew 6:21 reminds us, "For where your treasure is, there your heart will be also."* If you really want to know if someone really loves you, check out their priority list. If you are the last person on their list, you have gotten your answer. You do not need anyone to tell you what that means.

Be devoted to your relationship with your family. I encourage you to invest in love wisely. Our days are short and there is no time to waste doing foolish things. Invest in things that will make your family and friends proud. Enjoy your family and friends, and try to get along with the people around you. Remember, if someone dislikes or hates you, just know it may be how they perceive and see themselves. Do not take it personally. Do not lose your identity just because you are waiting for someone to love or affirm you. I have chosen to stay in love despite the hate in the world and around me. I will remain in love because it makes God happy, and it makes me happy as well.

- Love is patient.
- Love is kind.
- Love covers a multitude of sins.
- Love does not envy.
- Love is not proud.
- Love is not easily angered.
- Love is not rude.

- Love is not selfish.

- Love never gives up.

- Love crosses all boundaries.

- Love is humble.

- Love is caring for those who do not deserve it.

- Love never fails.

David, the greatest songwriter, wrote in *Psalm 18:1-2: "I love you, Lord God, and you make me strong. You are my mighty rock, my fortress, my protector, the rock where I am safe, my shield, my powerful weapon, And my place of shelter."*

Thank you, Lord, for your wonderful and unfailing love to me and my household. If I had many tongues, it would not be enough to thank you! But I thank you anyway with everything that is within me. Thank you, O Lord!

Chapter 2

TRUST MATTERS

Trust is an essential element in a relationship, whether it is a relationship with your spouse, family, friends or with God. If we must serve and obey God, we must first trust Him. The question is, can God be trusted? Well, I am here to openly declare to you that yes, God can be trusted! So, what is trust? How do we trust God and what does it look like to really trust God? The Oxford English Dictionary defines trust *as a "firm belief in the reliability, truth, ability, or strength of someone or something."* When we have trust and confidence in someone, we worry less and we get a sense of security and peace. When we look up to God and depend on Him for all our needs, we demonstrate to Him and those around us that our faith and trust is in God. It is important to settle the issue of trust with God before we can go deeper in Him. Many times, we worry about whether or not we can really trust God with our lives and circumstances. But, if the issue of trust is not settled, we will find ourselves worrying about our lives, children, families, and everything pertaining to life. Lack of trust can create anxiety, depression, restlessness and hopelessness. So, trust is a vital ingredient to live a peaceful and happy life.

VULNERABLE TRUST

I grew up in a trustworthy environment. As a child, I saw and felt the tender care and love my parents gave to my siblings and me. This gave me security and the ability to trust others, which also transferred to my relationship with God. Having a trusting relationship requires you to be open and to be true to yourself, which, of course, makes you vulnerable. Many people today have issues with trust for one good reason or another. The feeling has been transferred to our relationship with God as well. Since some of us cannot trust the people around us, we certainly feel we cannot trust the God whom we do not see. But trust is essential if we are to live a fruitful and happy life.

The question remains: Why do we live our lives as if God does not exist? Could it be because we cannot see, feel, or touch God? Or perhaps, it is easier to put our trust in humans than in God because we obtain instant gratification from speaking to people whether they are able to help us or not. Just because God is invisible does not mean He cannot hear us, touch us, or help us with our circumstances. Difficult moments and hardship should push us to seek hope and trust in God especially when we do not have any evidence to affirm our future. Proverbs 3:5-6 instructs us to *"Trust in the Lord with all your heart and lean not on to your own understanding; in all your ways submit to him and he will make your path straight".* Our problems are not bigger than God. We must humble ourselves, be vulnerable, and submit to God.

COMPLETE TRUST

How do we trust God, and what does it look like to really trust him? A few years ago, I attended a camp meeting at a church. The guest preacher shared the word of God. At the time, I was going through some rough times in my marriage, and I was broken. As he began to preach, suddenly the Holy Spirit spoke to me and said, "Trust me. Trust me with your pains." I responded, "LORD I trust you." He said, "Trust me COMPLETELY." Immediately, I understood what He meant. I actually was not trusting God completely, despite thinking I was. Giving God a part of my life while I held the rest was clearly not good enough. He wanted me to depend on Him completely. God wants us to depend on Him completely no matter the circumstances. He knows us better than we know ourselves and our situations. He wants to help us with whatever it is we are going through.

This was a valuable lesson for me to learn. The word COMPLETELY did it for me. Not only did I realize I had a problem submitting all my problems to God, but I also had issues submitting myself completely to God. Many of us are good at allocating our problems to various people in our lives instead of submitting to our problems and turning to God for help.

29

God sees beyond what you can see. Why not trust Him? We can trust God by believing and standing on His written words, fixing our eyes on Him, and following His instructions. Placing your trust in God's strength and sovereignty is an excellent way to live your life. Only God can make the alterations that are needed in your life for you to succeed.

Isaiah 55:8-9 says, *"For my thoughts are not your thoughts, neither are your ways my ways, declares the Lord. As the heavens are higher than the earth, so are my ways higher than your ways and my thoughts than your thoughts."* We must learn to trust God with our problems, big or small. God is bigger than our thoughts and the ideas of all humans combined.

OBEDIENT TRUST

One day, I drove to pick up my son from a basketball game. I got stuck in traffic and I became anxious as the cars barely moved. I became very worried about not being on time. Suddenly, I had this impression to make a u-turn and take another route to avoid the delay in reaching my son on time. As I was about to do so, I heard this gentle voice say to me, stay on the course. Recognizing it was the voice of the Holy Spirit, I got upset and started venting about my problems. Because for a while God had told me to be still and trust Him. As I continued to run my mouth, immediately, the voices ceased and there was silence. For some weird reason, I decided to stay on the course because I wanted to prove God wrong. How foolish? Who am I to try to prove God wrong? However, I stayed on the journey to see the outcome of these painful instructions. Mind you, I only had 30 minutes to pick up my son. The traffic before me was long as far as I could see, but what I failed to realize at the time was God's eyes saw beyond what I could see. As soon as I came through the ramp, there was a large pool of water that flooded the area to the stop sign. As I approached the stop sign, I realized the flood ended right there, but I thought the traffic was longer because I could only see but so far.. Our problems are not bigger than God, and we need to start seeing things through God's eyes and not our own. God knows what is in front of us. So, stay the course, and see what God can do!

It took me about 10 minutes to get to that stop sign, but it seemed like it was forever. I was able to pick up my son right on time. God is always on time. Sometimes in life, when we worry about our troubles, and sufferings, it may seem like God does not see or hear us. But, God *can* hear us, and He sees the details of our problems. He is going to bring us out of it. I had to go through this life experience for God to teach me that it was vital for me to trust in Him to develop a strong and sustainable relationship with Him. A relationship without trust is like a rope with one cord that can easily be broken when the high winds and storms of life come. Trust is necessary for a relationship to blossom. It is like a strong adhesive that holds a relationship together, and without it, relationships can easily fall apart. In every good relationship, trust is first established, followed by honesty, respect and open communication. This is what is required from us.

An amazing thing happened on the day I picked up my son from his basketball game. As I pulled up to the stop sign, there was no car in front of me. I heard a gentle voice say to me, "Your life is about to become like this journey." I broke down and started crying so hard. Tears ran down my cheeks. I could not contain myself. I was overwhelmed by the love of God. He was assuring me that although I was going through tough times, my journey with hard times was about to come to an end. His words gave me peace and comfort. Knowing that God was concerned about me and working things out for me made me happy. My spirit was lifted up. Our God is kind, compassionate, faithful and trustworthy. Thereafter, I asked for God's forgiveness for not trusting Him in the first place. I asked Him to teach me how to trust in Him completely. Psalm 37:18 *says, "Those who obey the Lord are daily in his care, and what he has given them will be theirs forever."* I trusted the Lord by relinquishing my control of things into His perfect hands. It is imperative that we trust God and allow Him to lead us and help us through our daily lives. All we need to do is be patient and trust God. If something troubles you, talk it over with God. When you are in despair, relax in the awesome hand of God, and put your energy and focus on trusting God. Rest in His presence. I urge you to trust God's love and faithfulness.

PEACEFUL TRUST

Many years ago, I was seven months pregnant when I developed high blood pressure and my doctor requested I be admitted to the hospital for monitoring. Later that night, I experienced severe abdominal pains with projectile vomiting, and I was immediately rushed to the operating room to deliver the baby by C-section. I was diagnosed with preeclampsia with HELLP (Hemolysis, elevated liver enzymes, low platelet count) syndrome. Thirty hours after delivery, my baby died from respiratory complications. Unfortunately, I had not seen my baby before his death because I was seriously ill. When I realized my baby was gone, my condition worsened. My heart was ripped apart, and I was in so much pain, especially when I realized I would be going home empty handed. At the time, my oldest daughter was two years old. I asked God to heal me because I knew my daughter needed me. The doctor came to my room to inform me I would need a blood transfusion. Later that day, the nurse started the blood transfusion. During the blood transfusion, the nurse called the doctor because she thought I was having a reaction to the blood transfusion because I spiked a fever minutes after starting the process. The doctors immediately stopped the transfusion. At this point, my kidneys were failing due to lack of blood volume.

Later that evening, the nurse started another blood transfusion. I was very scared. I prayed to God to send me a caring nurse and doctor to take care of me, and He certainly did! I laid down in bed facing the entrance to my hospital room when I saw a doctor walk slowly into my room. As he entered, he walked straight toward me. He never said a word to me. I was so weak; I could not lift my head to see or speak to him. There was something unusual about the doctor's white coat that caught my attention, and the way he walked into the room as if he was a secret agent, gently placing one foot in front of the other. His white coat was closer to his ankle. Surprisingly, when the doctor came close to the head of my bed, an overwhelming peace came over me, and I fell asleep, not waking up until midnight. When I did, I saw a nurse sitting at the foot of my bed doing her paperwork. I felt protected and safe. I realized God had answered my prayers so I went back to sleep. My healing process began that day. This experience catapulted my faith to a higher level. I knew I was not alone. God was with me through that difficult season of my life.

PROMISING TRUST

After 20 days in the hospital, I was discharged home. I began to grieve. I cried a lot and asked God why He took my son?

One morning as I began to ask God why he took my son away from me, He instructed me to open the Bible, but never said what book of the Bible or verse. Even in my sadness and anger, I decided to obey God. I placed my Bible on my lap, with my eyes closed, I opened the Bible to 1 Samuel chapter 2, and I began to read. 1 Samuel 2:6 caught my attention, which states, *"You take away life, and you give life. You send people down to the world of the dead and bring them back again."* Instantly, I stopped crying. I understood the LORD gave me the child, and He took him away. The entire page talked about a woman named Hannah who had no children and went to the house of God to ask God for a child. The prophet Eli saw her and thought she was drunk. Hannah told the prophet she was not drunk but was asking God for a child. Priest Eli told her not to worry because she would have a baby boy next year, and his name will be called Samuel because she asked the LORD for him. As soon as I finished reading the story, the Spirit of the LORD said to me, "I will give you a son, and you will call his name Samuel." I received the word and trusted God's promise to me.

Two years later, I gave birth to my son just as God had spoken. But, the enemy wanted to interrupt my delivery. I remembered during his delivery, I had pushed twice, the baby's heart rate dropped, and the doctor warned if the baby is not delivered after my third push, I would have to have a C-section. I really did not want to go through that again after my last traumatic experience. I prayed and asked God to please help me. As the next contraction came, I started to push forcefully, but something miraculous happened. Suddenly, I felt like someone bypassed my effort in pushing and I could not feel the exertion of my push! Although I was pushing, it felt like I was not. While I was trying to figure out what was going on in my head, I heard a baby's cry. The baby was delivered! When the baby was given to me for bonding, I was in awe of God's faithfulness and love. I sang praises to the LORD. Everything I dreamt of was before my eyes. My heart was filled with Joy. You asked, can God be trusted? I say yes, a big fat yes! God can be trusted!

CONFIDENT TRUST

What do you want or are in need of? Do you want a child? Do you need a job? Do you want a husband? Do you want a house? Do you need a car? Whatever your needs are, I want you to know, you can trust God for it. He is a good gift giver! Believe and you will see the goodness of God come through in your life.

People will try to make you doubt God. Do not worry, stay focused, and keep your eyes on Jesus. Trusting God is a process! As you continue to walk with God closely, you will learn to trust Him one day at a time. He will continue to empower and equip you to build your *trust muscles* as you go through life. As you win more victories, your trust level will continue to rise. Do not forget what He did for you in the past, and He will help you continue to win more battles. Matthew 6:34 says, *"Therefore do not worry about tomorrow, for tomorrow will worry about itself. Each day has enough trouble of its own."* Why worry when you can trust God and pray? Through all my life experiences, I have developed unwavering trust in God, and I have come to a place of rest with Him. Whenever I find myself worrying or anxious about anything, I take a step back and submit the issue to God by trusting and resting in Him to make things work out for my good.

In times of confusion and fear, I bring my uncertainties to Jesus, leave them at His feet, and walk away with His peace. The moment I recall His goodness, it reminds me that God is on His throne watching over me and my household. I give Him thanks because He has never failed me once. Philippians 4:6-7 says, *"Do not be anxious about anything, but in everything, by prayer and petition, with thanksgiving, present your requests to God. And the peace of God, which transcends all understanding, will guard your hearts and your minds in Christ Jesus."* To get the answers to our problems, we must first bring them to the LORD and ask God for His help, otherwise our situation will remain unchanged.

TIMELY TRUST

There have been times when God was silent when I prayed and asked Him for something. But, that does not mean He did not hear me. So, what happens when God is silent? Do you still trust Him? The story of Lazarus in John chapter 11 is a good example. Jesus was friends with Lazarus and his sisters Mary and Martha. When Lazarus was ill, his sisters called for Jesus to come and heal him. They were expecting Jesus to at least say a word of prayer to heal Lazarus. Afterall, they have seen for themselves the healing power Jesus carried when he spoke healing words to the Centurion's servant who was sick to death and was healed. Jesus assured Mary and Martha not to worry because Lazarus was going to be fine. Jesus did not show up before Lazarus died, nor did He pray for Lazarus to be healed. Jesus was silent! Lazarus died and Jesus showed up four days later.

Have you ever wondered why God was silent in some of your situations? Why didn't he fix your problems right away? Well, could it be because He wanted to get your attention? Maybe He wanted to teach you to be patient and trust in Him. Could it be because He wanted you to be closer to Him? Or, maybe He wanted His name to be glorified like He did in the case of Lazarus. How do we respond when God is silent? I am sure we run through a variety of emotions like disappointment, emptiness, confusion, anger, grief or disbelief. No matter what we feel, we need to remember Gods' silence does not always mean denial or rejection. Even King David, a man after God's own heart, was troubled, and he wondered if God heard his prayers when he said in Psalm 22:1-2, *"My God, my God, why have you forsaken me? Why are you so far from saving me, so far from my cries of anguish? My God, I cry out by day, but you do not answer, by night, but I find no rest."* How should we respond when God is silent? Asking God why does not guarantee you an answer. So, we must learn to trust Him, and respect God's right to be silent. While you wait on God, read and meditate on His word, cultivate a closer relationship with Him, stay prayed up, and rest in Him. He will come through in *His* time so that His name is glorified like in the case of Lazarus. Jesus called Lazarus from the grave back to life. Get ready as God prepares to call you out from your graves. God is about to do a new thing in your life!

Some of us have been conditioned to expect immediate answers not only from the people around us but from God as well. And when we cry out to God and nothing happens, we feel isolated, empty, and abandoned. Although it may seem like the door is shut and bolted, remember that God hears you, He cares about you, and He will respond and answer you when he deems it appropriate. On the other hand, God can say *"no"* and deny us access to our request. This is because He knows what is best for us better than we do. Learn to embrace God's silence. After all, who can question God or fault Him? He is God all by Himself.

When you candidly bring your prayer requests before God, be rest assured that He has heard your prayers, just like He did for Hannah and me. Isaiah 59:1 says, *"Surely the arm of the LORD is not too short to save, nor His ear too dull to hear."* Yes, He has ears. He can hear us! 1 John 5:14-15 says, *"This is the confidence we have in approaching God: that if we ask anything according to his will, he hears us. And if we know that he hears us -whatever we ask- we know that we have what we asked of him."* I encourage you to put your trust in the Lord and grab hold of the fact that God's eyes are on you, and He will wipe your tears and answer your prayers. Therefore, let us continue to pray without wavering. Prayer is your spiritual weapon. Use it.

God answered Hannah's prayers just as He answered my prayers, too, and gave me a son. Prophet Eli was close to God, and he knew the character of God and what God could do. We need to develop a close relationship with God, so that we can learn to trust God as well. Go ahead and declare His words and see the manifestations of your prayers come to fruition. God is calling out to you. I pray you make the right decision to answer his invitation and affirm your trust in Him, regardless of how you feel or what you are going through. You will not regret your decision to follow Him.

There were times in my life when I came to a fork in the road. I had to decide which road to take. When I did not know what to do, the Holy Spirit would direct me and give me peace on which way to follow. Some of the paths led to resolution of some problems, while others led to mountains which I had to climb. But through it all, God gave me the strength and power to overcome my problems. Whenever I got tired, He would stretch out His hands and pull me forward. There is always something better on the other side of that obstacle you are facing. Do not give up. Stay on the journey.

I have come to appreciate the difficult moments of my life because it was through these challenges and trials that I developed my confidence and faith in God. Look back on your life and recognize how God was present in your situation and how He helped you through tough times. God remains true to Himself throughout eternity. This is the basis of my confidence and trust in God.

I feel the urge to pray right now. Father in the name of Jesus Christ, for anyone who is reading this book and has a particular need that is dear to their heart, I ask that you bring it to pass now in the name of Jesus Christ, Amen!

Chapter 3

THE POWER OF FORGIVENESS

Forgiveness is a beautiful thing. God loves and treasures forgiveness. What is forgiveness? The Oxford English Dictionary defines it as *the action or process of forgiving or being forgiven.* Forgiveness is letting go of the offenses or painful acts or grudges toward someone. When we are afflicted by so many offenses, we find ourselves entangled with the spirit of unforgiveness and hate. Over time, we become angry, resentful, and unpleasant toward the people who wrong us. Sometimes, we even feel the urge to seek revenge because we are humans.

Forgiveness is an intentional process of freeing yourself from hurt and pains inflicted onto you. To let go of unforgiveness, you must be willing to let go of those who have wronged you to release your bitterness and hurt. The act of forgiveness is something that requires God's grace. We need the grace of God to help us forgive those who have abused, betrayed and hurt us. Forgiveness does not mean forgetting or excusing the wrong that was done to us. Neither is it associated with the person who caused you the pain. The process of forgiveness simply comes with the understanding that you are a sinful creature who may have offended others, and for this reason, you are willing to let go of the wrongdoings done toward you just as God has forgiven you of your sins toward Him. Forgiveness frees you from the grip of the offender and sets your soul free from bondage, allowing the peace and love of God to envelop you and reign in your life.

The Lord's prayer indicates that forgiveness is a vital element. Here is the Lord's Prayer in Matthew 6: 9-13:

"Our father in heaven, help us to honor your name.

Come and set up your kingdom, so that everyone on earth will obey you,

As you are obeyed in heaven.

Give us our food for today.

Forgive us for doing wrong as we forgive others.

Keep us from being tempted and protect us from evil."

"If you forgive others for the wrongs they do to you, Your Father in heaven will forgive you. But if you don't forgive others, your father will not forgive your sins."

The Lord's prayer instructs us to forgive others as God has forgiven us. But if we remain stubborn and hold on to unforgiveness and bitterness, then we have judged ourselves and given God the right not to forgive us of our own sins and offenses towards Him and others.

In my early Christian walk, I held on to grudges for the longest time against my offenders. One day, I read the book of Ecclesiastes 7:9, which says, *"Anger dwells in the bosom of fools."* I had to face and accept my own truth. I prayed to God for strength and grace to overcome the stronghold of unforgiveness. Although anger is a natural and normal emotion to feel when we have been hurt or mistreated, we should not stay angry for a long time. Ephesians 4:26 says, *"Be angry, yet do not sin. Do not let the sun go down on your anger."* In other words, it is ok to be angry about something because we are human. But staying angry for days and years can lead to sinful actions. It is destructive and harmful to our health.

Research has shown unforgiveness can affect not only our physical health, but also our psychological and spiritual health. I read an article from Johns Hopkins Medicine titled *"Forgiveness: Your Health Depends on It."* The article stated that unforgiveness can increase your risk of high blood pressure, cardiovascular disease, diabetes, and depression. In other words, if you forgive those who have mistreated you and deprived you of your peace and joy, you may lower your risk of the above-mentioned ailments. Chronic anger exposes you to a fight-or-flight mode which impacts your heart rate, blood pressure and your immune response. When you forgive those who have offended you, you can reduce your stress levels and reduce your risk of getting chronic diseases.

It is important that we do not let our past imprison us or steal our happiness and future. If we do not address the spirit of unforgiveness, it will rob us of our future, especially when we cannot change the past. There was a time in my life when I was consumed with the hurt others have caused me. The battle in my mind was endless and heavy. As soon as I tried to deal with one issue, another challenge popped up and the spirit of unforgiveness rose. Staying connected to God and His words was the best way I handled my problems. It was not easy. God began to convince me to forgive all those who had offended me. I told God I did not have the power and ability to forgive anyone. But, I was willing to move from my painful situation to something better. I was willing to do whatever it took, not fully understanding how to go about forgiving those who had mistreated me.

As time went by, the LORD began to gradually work in my heart. When I thought of my offenders, I no longer felt the pains, the resentment, and bitterness I once felt. I noticed God was molding and shaping my heart after His own heart. God had instructed me to forgive all those who had offended me so that He may bless me. He gave me the ability to do so because I was willing to let go. One evening, I began to call out the names of all those who had offended me and told God I forgave them. I mentally left them at the feet of Jesus and walked away a free woman. The burdens I had from carrying unforgiveness in my spirit disappeared, and the peace of God enveloped me and has never left me since.

God has a way of testing what we profess. Believe it or not, the next morning after the prayers of forgiving those who had offended me, as I walked from the parking garage to my office I saw one of my offenders walking toward me. The offender had never looked me in the eye or greeted me since our dispute. But, this very day as he got closer to me, he said, "Good morning, Tina!" My heart dropped into my stomach. Quickly, I responded back, "Good morning!" I recognized immediately that it was a test from God. With that experience, I confirmed to God that I meant everything I said the night before when I forgave all my offenders as He had directed me to. Proverbs 16:7 says, *"When a man's ways please the Lord, he makes even his enemies to be at peace with him."* My heart was filled with joy not only because I passed the test, but because I felt great afterward. I had no grievances or unsettled feelings like I used to have when I encountered him. It was the beginning of my freedom from all my offenders and haters.

Matthew 5:43-45 says, *"You have heard people say love your neighbors and hate your enemies. But I tell you to love your enemies and pray for anyone who mistreats you. Then you will be acting like your Father in heaven. He makes the sun rise on both good and bad people. And he sends rain for the ones who do right and for the ones who do wrong."* We must all show grace to one another by forgiving each other. What good is it if you love people who only love you? There is nothing good about it all. Therefore, we must humble ourselves before the LORD and learn to forgive others. Matthew 5:22 explains that if we are angry with someone, or call people worthless or a fool, that we will face trial and could be in danger of hell. So, let us try to be at peace with everyone to save ourselves from the judgment of God.

The spirit of unforgiveness can impact our health and well-being. A long time ago, I cared for a patient who was hospitalized for more than 20 days due to abdominal pains. She could not tolerate eating any type of food without having severe abdominal pains. She had an endoscopy that suggested possible intestinal ulcers. She was placed on intravenous Total Parenteral Nutrition (TPN) for nourishment, and intravenous medication to treat the ulcer. She was seen by a psychiatric doctor whose medical note revealed the patient stated she had been tormented by her late spouse's spirit and could not sleep at night. She also expressed many other emotional traumas that were inflicted on her by other people. Clearly, she was carrying the spirit of unforgiveness in her heart. In the medical field, we are not permitted to speak about our religious beliefs to our patients. However, I noticed she was wearing a crucifix necklace and felt, perhaps, she believed in Jesus Christ. So, I took a chance and I expressed how I loved her crucifix necklace. I sat at her bedside, and we began to talk about her health and what she had been dealing with for a while. She shared with me the painful abuse by loved ones, betrayals, and issues with family members. I sat and listened and was never judgmental. She later affirmed that she was a Christian. That information helped me to talk about what Jesus Christ would do with all her offenses and what He would like us to do. I shared with her how Jesus forgave us of our offenses and sins, and how Jesus wants us to do the same to those who have offended us. During our 45-minute conversation, she must have screamed about 10 times. The pain medications were not enough to relieve her severe abdominal pains.

After much discussion, it was time for us to pray. I instructed her to call out the names of the people who had offended her, to say I forgive you, to leave them at the feet of Jesus, and to walk away. At first, it was difficult for her to say the names of her offenders. We overcame that by pleading the blood of Jesus Christ after several trials. Finally, she named 12 people she held captive in her spirit that offended her. Then, we prayed a prayer of repentance and asked God for grace to help her forgive her offenders. To my greatest surprise, each day her abdominal pains began to improve with evidence of less screaming.

Four days later, I weaned her off the TPN because she was able to tolerate a soft diet. She also had no further dreams about her dead spouse tormenting her, and she was able to sleep through the night. This is the power of forgiveness. You can prevent disease and set yourself free from illness. Forgiveness is not for the offender; it is for you! Because she forgave those who had abused and hurt her, God restored her health. Matthew 6:14-15 says, *"If you forgive others for the wrongs they do to you, your Father in Heaven will forgive you. But if you don't forgive others, your father will not forgive your sins."* We must take this to heart and learn to forgive.

Sometimes, it is easy for us to condemn people. But, if we can see through God's eyes, we will realize we are not in any place to be the judge of others. Matthew 7:1-2 tells us not to condemn others, and God won't condemn us. *God will be as hard on us as we are on others! He will treat us exactly as we treat them.* This same chapter in verse 4 says we should be careful in trying to remove the speck out of our brother's eye when we have a log in our own eyes. Truthfully, many of us want to fix other people when we need a thorough cleansing ourselves. It is important for us to first examine ourselves and take time to address issues that are dragging us to the pit. Forgiveness does not equal or guarantee reconciliation because reconciliation may not be possible if the offender is dead or is unwilling to communicate.

It is not ok to take out your insecurities that stem from unforgiveness on your spouse, friends or family members. They are not your trash can where you dump all your insecurities, anger, and low self-esteem. They are human with their own issues, just like you. So, let us respect ourselves and each other, and take responsibility for our own problems. Seek help and address your issues. Some of us are good at sweeping our dirty attitudes and behaviors under the carpet instead of sweeping them out and cleaning after ourselves. Unfortunately, we cannot wish our problems away. Do not allow your own bitterness and hatred to make you become an enemy of yourself or to become a beast when you were made to be a prince or princess. Do not allow your own bitterness and inferiority complex to swallow you up like a raging sea. God loves you and wants to help you become the best version of yourself. Would you allow Him to help you?

Unforgiveness is like cancer. It slowly eats into the fabric of your soul until it destroys your life completely. I try not to be offended by others. But because I am human, when I find myself getting upset, I take a step back and remind myself it is not worth my life to carry offenses in my spirit. I tell myself to forgive, and right away my spirit is back at peace with God. There are surely so many benefits in forgiving those who have hurt us. Here are some benefits listed below:

- You develop a healthy relationship with people around you.
- You become less anxious and irritable.
- You avoid depression.
- You lower your blood pressure.
- You develop a stronger immune system.
- You promote your mental health.
- You improve your heart health.
- You improve your self-esteem and worth.
- You become a winner over unforgiving spirit!

What if the person you forgave does not change? Well, you do not own it. In other words, that is not your business. The offender's actions and behaviors are not yours to own. Forgiveness is about you and not the other person. Forgiveness gives you the power and authority to take your life back from the offender. It is vital that you first forgive yourself and avoid being harsh on yourself. Stop judging yourself. Jesus said to the woman caught in the act of adultery, "Where are the ones who condemn you?" In John 8: 1-11, *Some Pharisees brought a woman who had been caught in adultery to Jesus and they stated that the law of Moses says to stone such a person to death. They wanted to know what Jesus had to say about the situation. Then Jesus asked them, who among you is without sin, go ahead and cast the first stone. The woman's accusers, knowing that they have all sinned, slipped away one by one leaving Jesus and the woman alone. Jesus asked the woman, where are your accusers? And there was no one left. Jesus said, if no one condemns you, neither do I. Go and sin no more.* God is always waiting to forgive us of our sins. What should we do? We need to humble ourselves, repent of our sins, and surrender to God, and He will forgive us of our sins and empower us to forgive others.

In the book of Genesis, there is another great example of forgiveness in the life of Joseph. Joseph was the second youngest among his many brothers. He was his father's favorite son, and his father gifted him a special coat made of many colors. Joseph also had a close relationship with God, and God showed him what his future looked like in his dreams. Joseph would often get excited about his dreams and would share them with his family. His brothers became jealous and hateful toward him and eventually sold him into slavery. He was taken to Egypt and eventually became a slave to a captain of the Egyptian king's guard named Potiphar. While in Potiphar's house, he was accused of adultery and was sent to prison. While in prison, he had the opportunity to interpret the dreams of two men who had worked for Pharaoh. Years later, Pharaoh had a dream that nobody could interpret except Joseph. And, every word Joseph gave came to pass. Joseph was promoted, and he became second in command after Pharaoh. There was a famine in the land, and Joseph's family had to come to Egypt where there was plenty of food to get some grain for their family. Joseph saw his brothers for the first time since they sold him into slavery. However, his brothers did not recognize him. Nevertheless, his brothers eventually realized Joseph, the second commander in chief, was their little brother who they wronged long ago. They were afraid for their lives, but Joseph did not take revenge as they thought he would. Instead, he forgave them all, and he was reunited with his father and brothers again. Joseph said, although his brothers tried to harm him, God worked everything out for his good.

I have learned not to worry about my haters. As I look back on my life, I can see how God took my pain and brokenness and made a beautiful mosaic out of the ashes of my life. God is constantly reminding me of the great provision He has for my life. To achieve this purpose, I must learn to intentionally stay focused and trust the LORD to see His spoken words come to pass in my life, just like they did for Joseph. I am truly glad God has used my past to make something beautiful out of my life. What my enemies intended for evil, God has turned for good.

Psalm 32, 1-2 says, *"Blessed is the one whose transgressions are forgiven, whose sins are covered. Blessed is the one whose sin the Lord does not count against them and whose spirit is no deceit."* When we confess our sins without hiding it, God is faithful to forgive us. But when we refuse to repent of our sins, we remain in darkness and miss valuable lessons from God. But, if we are smart enough, we will openly receive God's corrections. Some of us do not care about what God says or what He thinks because evil has taken over our hearts, and we have become cold and callous. I am grateful that God took my sins, shame and guilt away. He gave me the power, confidence and strength to turn away from sin. For He has given us power and authority to rule over the earth and take it captive for our good and for His Glory.

If you are ready to forgive your offenders, ask God to empower you to forgive them, and He will give you the strength and the grace to do so. If you do not forgive, you may go down a slippery slope of no return – a path that is dark and can become darker as we hold on to an unforgiving spirit. You can change the trajectory of your life and move toward the light. Jesus, the light of the world, will lift you up and direct your path. Amen.

Chapter 4

STAYING CONNECTED

When I first became a Christian, I learned the habit of spending time with God and learned about His words and character. My early memories of connecting and building my relationship with God was purely through His grace and love for me. Over the years, spending time with God and staying connected with my Creator has been life-changing and pivotal to my success. I have learned that it is essential for me to stay connected to the triune God (God the Father, the Son, and the Holy Spirit).

I was in the 12th grade when I became a Christian. I had some Scripture Union Christians (a Christian group in Nigeria) at school who introduced me to God. These students were strong faithful believers who were fervent in prayer and in the word. As I began to learn the word of God with the group during school lunch breaks, I slowly began to fall in love with Jesus. I was eager to hear more about God the Father, Jesus Christ, and the Holy Spirit. I was so much in love with Jesus that I spent most of my time studying the word and talking with God.

To be a fruitful Christian, it is imperative to stay connected to God. How do you stay connected to God? I am glad you asked! First, you must identify yourselves. Who are you? It is important for us to know who we are and to whom we belong to help us stay connected with God. For me, I knew I was a child of God, created in God's image and likeness to do great works and worship Him. What about you? John 15: 4-6 says, *"Remain in me, and I will remain in you. No branch can bear fruit by itself; it must remain in the vine. Neither can you bear fruit unless you remain in me. I am the vine; you are the branches. If a man remains in me and I in him, he will bear much fruit; apart from me you can do nothing. If anyone does not remain in me, he is like a branch that is thrown away and withers; such branches are picked up, thrown into the fire, and burned."*

I see the kingdom of God like a tree of life. I see God the Father as the main root because He is the source of our life and existence. Jesus Christ is the vine that connects us to the Father. We are the branches attached to the Vine, and without the Vine we are lifeless. As a branch, we must be willing to take part in the family tree to be fully nourished and fruitful. Branches that fail to engage or participate in the activity of the family tree will eventually break off and die. We become fruitless when we refuse to nourish ourselves from the great Vine. When we stay connected to the Vine, we become like that tree planted by the river. Psalm 1:3 says, *"He shall be like a tree planted by the rivers of water, whose leaf shall not wither, and whatever he does shall prosper."* No matter the season of life, our leaves will never dry up, and our lives will never become barren of fruits.

Several years after I left Nigeria to move to the United States, my priority began to shift from spending more time with God to spending more time at work and caring for family. As most of us know, America is considered the land of great opportunities, especially for those who have dreams. So, having this great opportunity was exciting, and spending time with God became less important. That was the first huge error I made in my life. A mistake you do not want to make. Don't get me wrong, Jesus was still my Savior, and He never left my heart, but my focus was no longer on Him completely like it was when I was back in Nigeria. Life began to happen for me. I got married, graduated from nursing school, and started having children. With these wonderful life accomplishments came some struggles. There was not enough time for God. I began to feel empty as my spiritual tank depleted.

Have you ever been in a place in your life where you felt your situation was hopeless? There were seasons in my life when I felt there was no hope for me. But God allows moments like this to reconnect you to Himself. One day a guest speaker came to my church and spoke about how the issues of her life had pulled her away from God. I was drawn to her story because I was experiencing the same thing in my life. She shared that she was able to break the cycle of her lukewarm Christianity by waking up to pray at midnight after her family went to bed. She sacrificed her sleep to reconnect with God. I was so excited to hear her story. That very night I did just that. After I spent several weeks waking up at midnight to spend quality time with God, I began to feel closer again to the One who first loved me. James 4:8a says, *"Draw near to God and He will draw near to you."* There is hope!

Over the years, as my relationship became stronger, the LORD began to encourage me to tell people about Him. I told God I was not the right person, and I am not equipped to do so. After several years, I was invited to a church program that gave people who felt God had called them an opportunity to minister on any subject for 10 minutes. One after the other, the women came up to the stage and gave a word. Then came this vibrant, young lady on the stage. She began to break down the word of God. She was well spoken, charismatic and full of energy, and the whole room was electrified as she preached the gospel. Luckily for me, I was not picked to speak. Thank God!

At the end of her 10 minutes of preaching, I found all the reasons in the world to let God know why I could not preach the gospel just like that young girl. I told God she was the kind of person to represent His kingdom and preach the gospel. Before I could even finish my thoughts, the Holy Spirit interrupted me and said, "It is the anointing that breaks the yoke." I was cut short in my thoughts. How can there not be an anointing in what I just experienced? I realized from that moment we must be careful of the feel-good preaching. The preaching where we all get excited, but we are still empty and broken. The chains were shaken alright, but they were not broken, and people were still in bondage. God made me realize that it will not be my charisma or how well I speak that will get the job done. It is His Spirit that will do the work, and I will be the vessel. My goodness, what a relief!

When we come before the LORD with a sincere heart, He comes down to our level in the fullness of His glory, He heals our wounded souls, and He mends our broken hearts to nurture us back to life. After we are restored, we pay it forward. I was really humbled. I finally reached a conclusion that if the LORD was asking me to speak on his behalf, who am I to say no? I vowed to God that very day that I would trust Him and do whatever He asked me to do, but I would need His help. A few years later, I did my first healing conference. It was at this conference when I realized, indeed, God's anointing is what breaks the yoke. God's presence was tangible, and His anointing was present at the conference. People were physically and spiritually healed. Seeing that powerful move of God increased my faith and confidence that God was indeed calling me to come and dine with Him by preaching the gospel. And I accepted the call.

After holding the conference, I felt the God of Glory upon me for more than 24 hours. I was undone. When I came close to people that very day after the conference, they felt the power and presence of God. At night, I felt like I was surrounded by a warm fire and the feeling of warm oil being poured over me. I never wanted to leave the presence of God. But, I also knew I could not physically function if I carried that type of God's glory around me every day. It was a sweet, beautiful and humbling experience.

For everyone who has accepted Jesus Christ as their LORD and Savior, the Holy Spirit lives within you, and you have been given the authority to do good works with the LORD. Who is the Holy Spirit? The Holy Spirit is the third person of the Holy Trinity (Father, Son, and the Holy Spirit). He is our helper and mediator. He does most of the talking with the believer. He convicts us, He corrects us, and He directs us. The Holy Spirit is connected to the Father and the Son. They are inseparable. John 16:14 says, *"But when He, the Spirit of truth, comes, He will guide you into all truth. He will not speak on his own; He will speak only what He hears, and He will tell you what is yet to come."* John 5:19 says, *"Then answered Jesus and said unto them, verily, verily, I say unto you, The Son can do nothing of Himself, he can do only what he sees his Father doing, because whatever the Father does the Son also does."* Wow!

I had an experience one time in my early Christian walk. I was confused on how to pray. I always prayed to Jesus, in the name of Jesus. The moment I caught myself, I began to apologize to the LORD. The Spirit of the LORD encouraged me and said not to worry because when I spoke to Jesus, the Father and the Son heard me at the same time. Then I found peace. In *John 10:30, Jesus said, "I and the Father are one."* They are inseparable. The LORD's prayer taught us to pray to our Father who is in heaven. And, as stated in Colossians 3:17, we are also to pray through Jesus Christ to the Father because He is the sacrificial Lamb. It is through the shedding of His blood that allows us to stand before God to ask Him for anything. We could not have done it without His blood. In *2 Corinthians 5:21, "God made him who knew no sin to be sin for us, so that in him we might become the righteousness of God".* Jesus Christ is our Savior and Redeemer. This is the power of the cross. The power in the blood of Jesus has given us authority and dominion to cast out demons and to call things that are not as if they were. Philippians 2 :10 reads, *"So that at the name of Jesus every knee should bow, in heaven and on earth and under the earth."*

The fear of the LORD is the beginning of righteousness, wisdom and holiness. The Merriam-Webster Dictionary defines wisdom as the ability to discern inner qualities and relationships. It is the ability to make sound judgment. Wisdom is a gift from God. *James 1:5 says, "If any of you lack wisdom, you should ask God, who gives generously to all without finding fault, and it will be given to you."* Do you need wisdom? Ask God for it, and He will supply it. Just stay connected.

It is essential we learn about the fear of God. It was the fear of God that made Joseph refuse to commit adultery with Potiphar's wife. It was the fear of God that gave Abraham a willing heart to sacrifice his son, Isaac, as God directed him to, before God provided a ram as an offering instead. It was the fear of God that made Noah build the ark. It was the fear of God that made Job not curse God. Fearing the LORD does not mean we are to be afraid of Him. It means we respect and honor Him in all that we do. It is a reverence for His mighty power, His glory, His awesomeness, His wrath, and His anger. This is a healthy type of fear. Many of us today do not fear God, but we are afraid of God as if He is a beast or monster ready to devour us. He is NOT like that! He is a kind, compassionate, forgiving and loving God. We do not have to be afraid of God, but we must learn to revere His name. We respect God when we turn away from sin or anything that we know displeases Him. Take a moment and evaluate your life and see what behaviors and characters need to die. God will supply you with the grace and strength to make that change that is needed. We must be willing to nourish ourselves with the word of God, obey His instructions, and avoid destructive behaviors.

Psalm 25:12 reads, "Who are those who fear the Lord? He will show them the path they should choose." And verse 14 says, "The secret of the Lord is with those who fear him, and he will show them his covenant." When we fear the LORD, we show Him love, respect, appreciation, and honor. The fear of the LORD brings us great benefits.

- The fear of the LORD is key to knowledge.
- The fear of the LORD is key to divine wisdom.
- The fear of the LORD is key to understanding.
- The fear of the LORD is key to God's heart.
- The fear of the LORD brings peace
- The fear of the LORD brings eternal life.
- The fear of the LORD allows friendship with God.
- The fear of the LORD reveals the secrets of the Lord.
- The fear of the LORD hates evil.

We need to prioritize our relationship with God by putting God first in our lives. Matthew 6:33 says, *"But seek ye first the kingdom of God and his righteousness and all these things will be given to you as well."* It is essential to set apart time to regroup and recover in the spirit so we do not end up depleted, empty and lonely. Staying connected physically, emotionally and spiritually with the LORD is vital to our spiritual growth. We must be intentional about it. *Matthew 6:21 says, "For where our treasure is, there your heart will be also."* So, learn to stay connected to God, by spending time in His word, and in prayer. Stay away from sin, strife and unforgiveness. Be open and accept the Holy Spirit's correction, and you will never regret that you choose to stay connected to God.

Chapter 5

UNQUENCHABLE FAITH

I was the first person in my family to believe in the Lord Jesus Christ. When I was in the 12th grade, I was afflicted with a disease that was never diagnosed because my parents refused to take me to the hospital. When my younger brother was sick, they took him to the hospital, and three weeks later he died. They were afraid the same thing could happen to me. Instead, they took me to various native doctors for treatment. Unfortunately, none of the treatments were effective, until I received a supernatural healing from God.

After this painful experience, my entire family turned to God. Being in a Christian home taught me the importance of placing my trust and confidence in God and ways to handle life situations and conflicts. I gave my life to God when I was 17 years old, and I have never looked back. The Gospel of Jesus of Christ continues to have a great impact not only in my heart, but in the way I see the world and relate with people. The word faith is very important to me. When I was in my 20s, I heard the audible voice of God, and He said, "Your name shall be called faith." I am not exactly sure why He gave me that name, but all my life, I realized I have unexplainable faith and confidence in God.

Faith is an essential ingredient to secure what we believe about God. No matter your religion, you will need faith or confidence to believe what that religion teaches. Whether we know it or not, we have all been given a measure of faith. *Hebrews 11: 6 states, "Without faith it is impossible to please God. Anyone who wants to come to Him must believe that God exists and that he rewards those who sincerely seek Him."*

So, what is faith? The Merriam-Webster Dictionary defines faith as *complete trust or confidence in someone or something. Or a strong belief in God or in the doctrine of a religion, based on spiritual apprehension rather than proof. Hebrews 11:1 defines faith as, "The assurance of things hoped for, the conviction of things not seen."* In other words, faith is believing in something you do not have evidence to prove. The very day I accepted Jesus as my LORD and Savior, I believed every word written in the Bible with every ounce of my being. I try to honor the word of God, and I have no doubt concerning His words. If He said it, I believe it. Period! I am where I am today because of my unwavering faith in God. Everything I do revolves around God. This is not only because I know Him, but because I love Him, and I trust Him completely.

As I reflect on my life's journey, my trials, tests and struggles have given me the opportunity to develop and grow my faith. Do you know faith and trust go hand in hand? To trust someone, you must first have faith in them. When people are unfaithful, it is difficult to trust them. This is one reason why many marriages fail today. In every relationship, it is essential to establish trust. Trust is the foundation upon which a relationship is built. It is one of the strongest elements needed to maintain a healthy relationship and marriage.

I see faith as a gift from God to all people. Yes, even unbelievers have faith. Romans 12:3 shows *that God has given us a measure of faith.* Humans can believe something if they want to believe it or not. Roman 10:17 says, *"So then faith cometh by hearing, and hearing by the word of God."* Faith is what gives us the confidence and boldness to come into God's presence, to seek His face, and to ask and believe God for something. It is the measurement of my faith that deepens my relationship with God and helps me to move forward with the things that matter, not only to me, but to God as well. Every victory and failure of my life has strengthened my faith in God.

When I got pregnant with my youngest daughter, Nosa, my faith and trust were tested. We were already blessed with two wonderful children, so my husband and I had decided not to have any more babies, especially considering my awful morning sicknesses during my pregnancies. However, my oldest daughter and my son often told me they wanted another sibling. They would nag and beg me to get another baby, as if I could just go to the marketplace to buy one. To respond to their request, I would tell them to pray to God for another baby. Mind you, I was taking every precaution to not get pregnant. On my 40th birthday, my husband threw me a birthday party. A month later, I found out I was pregnant. "How could this be?" I asked myself. I almost had a heart attack. First, I was afraid to tell my husband. Then I thought to myself, he is the cause of this trouble. So, I told him about the pregnancy, and he said, "I am too old for this!" Frankly, I was not ready to go through the long months of morning sickness and misery. With all this thought going through my mind, I began to think of the unthinkable - an abortion.

I know God does not approve of abortions, but because I had a fear of dying by carrying the baby, I thought my only option was to get an abortion. So, I made an appointment with the family parenthood clinic for the procedure. Two days before the appointment, I called a close family friend and told her of my plight. To my greatest surprise, she said "Tina, you are a woman of God, I know if you pray about it, God will tell you what to do." Immediately, something grabbed my heart, and I felt my faith rising. Then, I said to God, "You have two days to speak to me otherwise, I have no other option than to move forward with the procedure." Looking back, who was I to give God an ultimatum?

I got home from work that night and found a quiet place in the house with my Bible in my hand. I began to pray. I must have fallen asleep twice or more between my prayers. It was almost 1 a.m., and I continued to pray because my life depended on it. I fell asleep again, but that time was different. Suddenly, I felt a hand tap on my right thigh twice. I woke up. When I opened my eyes, I was expecting to see my husband, but to my greatest surprise, there was nobody in the room. Instead, I heard a loud voice say, "Matthew 2:14." I remember resounding the verse, but I fell back to sleep because I was so tired. When I woke up that morning at 6:30 a.m., I was worried I had not gotten any revelation. Then, immediately, I heard the voice again with great emphasis yelling, "Matthew 2:14!" My ribs began to quiver, filled with anxiety and fear of what the LORD would have me to do. Quickly, I took my Bible from the nightstand and turned to *Matthew 2:14. It reads, "And so he took the mother and the child and escaped to Egypt."* At first, I was shocked because the verse was talking about a mother and a child. But wait. Where am I escaping to? I was so confused! But God is not an author of confusion. Nevertheless, I knew God had heard me. But, what was the meaning of the verse?

As I was driving back from work the next day feeling sad and frustrated about what that scripture meant, suddenly, I heard a gentle voice instructing me to read the verse before. You would have thought I should have done that, but I did not until I was given these instructions by God. So, I got home and read *Matthew 2:13. And it says, "After the wise men had gone, an angel of the Lord appeared to Joseph in the dream at night and said, Get up! Hurry and take the child and his mother to Egypt! Stay there until I tell you to return, because Herod is looking for the child and wants to kill him."* Immediately, the overwhelming peace of God fell upon me, and my fears instantly disappeared. I finally got the message, do not kill the child! I accepted God's words, and my plan for abortion was out the window. One word from God can change your entire life for good.

Did you know that during this pregnancy I had no morning sickness? The hand of God was upon my life. Everywhere I went people said I was a beautiful pregnant woman. I would chuckle, because I knew they were observing the glory of God upon my life. This is the God I have come to know. He is a faithful God.

Are you ready to surrender your situations to God? Many times, we give up easily and settle for less than what God has planned for us. Do not give up because God is not done with you yet. Allow Him to speak into your life because He has the final word over you. Do not be afraid. Let the God who created you rescue you from all your troubles. When you cross deep rivers, it will not drown you. When you walk through fire, it will not consume you. He will teach you how to climb mountains, swim out of the deep raging waters, and help you soar like an eagle. God wants to promote you to your next level, but you are afraid to take the leap of faith to your next destination. Do not be afraid, have faith, trust God, and jump over your hurdles because it is going to be ok if you stay connected to God and have faith.

If your past is dragging you and preventing you from reaching your best self, confront your issues, and address them. Do not sweep anything under the rug. If you do not address your issues, they will stop you from moving forward. The power to take the past and leave it in the past is in your hands. Remember, your past does not define you. Do not worry about what people would say about you. It does not matter what people say. You and God are the drivers of your life. So, do not hand your life to someone else to dictate how your life should be. Take matters into your own hands and run to Jesus with all your issues. He is waiting to help you with your problems. You cannot change the past, but you can define what your future should be like with the guidance of the Holy Spirit.

Some of you have been carrying grievances and hurt for a long time. You need to let go, so that God can fill your life with His blessings. My past used to suck the life out of me. It stole my joy and left me empty. I felt like the devil was sitting by my bedside daily waiting to resume the conversations of my problems in my head. Isaiah 43:19 was my go-to *Scripture.* *"Forget what happened long ago! Don't think about your past. I am creating something new. There it is! Do you not see it? I have put roads in deserts, streams in thirsty lands."* God is indeed faithful. This Scripture came out to be true in my life. I left everything that has caused me pain at the feet of Jesus and picked up His love, compassion, and grace. God does not want you holding onto grudges and hurt in your heart because it prevents you from getting your blessings. There is no time to waste. Let go of your past and grab hold of your bright and amazing future that God has prepared for you from the time of your birth.

Remember, you are dear to God's heart, He loves you, and He has chosen you for Himself. I am glad that God Almighty has chosen me! Who am I that God is mindful of me? I am forever grateful. Believe me, you may not know or see where God is taking you with your physical eyes, but trust and have faith in God, and He will open your spiritual eyes and understanding to see what He sees for your future. 1 Corinthians 2:9 says, *"No eyes have seen, no ears have heard or have entered the heart of men, the things God has prepared for those who love Him."* God has the master plan for your life.

Do you know I had no plans of becoming a nurse practitioner until God revealed it to me? Although I was not mentally ready for it, God encouraged me and gave me the strength to start and complete the program with flying colors, all because I followed God's instructions and plans.

Have faith in God, and you will begin to see greater things come through in your life. If you want to excel in life, I encourage you to stay connected to God, and you will be fruitful. There will be times when God will say no to your request, be prepared to accept His no's because it is part of the process.

There is power in the word of God. *Hebrews 4:12 says, "For the word of God is alive and active. Sharper than any double-edged sword, it penetrates even to divide soul and spirit, joints, and marrow; it judges the thoughts and attitudes of the heart."* If God has spoken over your life, I dare you to have faith and trust in Him to bring His words to pass in your life. You will never regret putting your faith in God.

One evening, I was lying down in my bedroom pondering on the word faith. I instantly asked the Holy Spirit what it meant to really have faith. Suddenly, the word FAITH was decoded as *Feeling Authorized In The Heavenly*. I was like wait, LORD! I began to get a download of knowledge. Whenever we find ourselves standing under an open heaven – being in the presence and power of God - the Holy Spirit fills us with this authority to call things to earth from the heavenly realm. Then I recalled several times when I was under open heavens how I felt the Spirit of God rising in me to do things I never envisioned doing in my life.

I once took care of a patient who was diagnosed with colon cancer, and she was given six months to live. When I approached her room one day, she and her daughter were holding hands and crying. I was deeply touched and empathetic about her prognosis. After a while, I asked her about her faith in an attempt to call a chaplain. Then the patient responded, "I used to believe in God, but I don't need any chaplain." "Well," I said, "This may be the time to return back to God." I encouraged her to stay strong.

As I was about to leave her room, the Spirit of the LORD instructed me to pray with her. The first thing that came to my mind was a question. LORD, you want me to pray with her? She has six months to live! Suddenly, I felt authorized in the heavenly realm and the atmosphere of the room changed. I obeyed the voice and turned back to the room to pray with her. I prayed under the guidance of the Holy Spirit for God's healing hand to touch her. As I walked out of the patient's room, the Spirit of the LORD told me to get her phone number. So, I went back and got her phone number. When I finally got out of her room, I was short on words and could not explain what took place in that room. Then, I asked the Holy Spirit, "Why did you ask me to get her phone number?" He said, "How would you know if I healed her?"

I was shocked and happy at the same time. Due to my own fears and some unbelief, I waited close to six months before I gave her a call. The first time I called there was no answer. I called three different times, and no one answered. My little faith plummeted. I began to question why God asked me to pray for her when He knew she was going to die! I was so disappointed and upset. But after a while, I accepted that she was dead and found comfort that she was with God because she reconnected to Him before she was discharged from the hospital.

Two years later, I walked into my unit. The unit secretary said a patient was admitted from the operating room last night and she was looking for me. I asked what the patient's name was, and she told me. I ran into the room, and it was the patient who was given six months to live! She saw me and screamed, "Tina! My doctor said I am a miracle woman!" I could not believe my eyes. I started crying because I did not have enough faith to trust God's words. It was tears of joy and the realization that God can be trusted no matter the situation. She was cancer free! She came back to the operating room to take down her ileostomy. Ever since, my faith tripled. From that day on, no matter the outcome of a situation, I stay true to God and hold on to His unfailing words.

I encourage you to examine yourself and learn to develop your faith. Start building your faith by reminding yourself of the faithfulness of God in your life. Reflect on His provision, protection and promises, and trust God's plan for you. Follow God's instructions, and surrender your will to His will. Allow Him to stretch and build your faith muscles. Then, you will see God's power and glorious manifestations in your life.

When things seem to be going wrong in your life and you lose control over your circumstances, trust God and have faith in Him. The Holy Spirit who is near to you will be ready to offer you the help you need. You will find true joy when you depend on God to move your insurmountable mountains. Following the lead of the Holy Spirit is key to our victories. 2 Corinthians 5:7 says, *"For we walk by faith and not by sight."* Your faith is your weapon. It empowers you to fight and win all your battles. You are an overcomer!

Chapter 6

HEARING FROM GOD

In my early walk with God, I did not realize God could speak, but I had the feeling He could hear. A year or so after I accepted Jesus Christ as my Savior, I started to hear Him speak to me audibly. Moments after He told me something, it would happen, and it began to grab my attention. Overtime, I became familiar with the voice of God. That said, it is important to know that the devil can also try to imitate God's voice, so you must be very careful and test all spirits to be sure it is God speaking to you.

Hearing from God is a necessity for believers if we are to walk in God's perfect will for us. It is vital we learn how to hear from God. When we are making significant life decisions, it is essential to consult with God, the one who knows our past, our present and our future. So many of us today gamble with our lives when we should be intentional and focused on what God has to say about our life situations and circumstances. We gamble with our lives when we depend on external factors to deal with our life issues. Many of us seek the opinions of friends, family, social media, sorcerers, religious leaders, and other sources when we should first go to God with our problems. Our

God is a good Father, and He is always speaking to His children. But, most of us cannot hear Him. God desires to speak with His children, just as our earthly parents desire to speak with us. Jeremiah 29:11 says, *"For I know the thoughts that I have towards you, saith the Lord, thoughts of peace, and not of evil, to give you an acceptable end."* God's plan for our lives is way better than ours. I have many life experiences to prove it.

Isaiah 30:21 says, *"Whether you turn to the right or the left, your ears will hear a voice behind you, saying, this is the way; walk in it."* To hear from God, we must develop a close relationship with Him so we can be familiar with his voice. The more we stay closer to the LORD, the better we are able to recognize his voice from other voices. It also requires us to be intentionally focused and to be attentive to hear from Him. Isaiah 55:3 tells us to *"Incline our ears to God so that our soul may live."* When we hear from God, our marital lives and relationships with others blossom. Our businesses, jobs, and other life encounters thrive because hearing from God can deliver us from many troubles. How? God will give you instructions and guidance to choose the best path for your life. Now, that does not mean you will not encounter challenges in life. But when you do, you can get directions from the Spirit of God on what to do.

Hearing from God is a daily practice, and it takes time. It is like infants learning to recognize the voices of their parents. As they grow older, they become familiar with their parents' voices. If you are in a crowd and your mother or father begins to call out your name, no matter how noisy the crowd may be, you will recognize the voice of your parents. This is the type of relationship our heavenly Father wants with us – for us to become one with God the Father, Son and the Holy Spirit. Remember, it takes time to learn to differentiate the voice of God from other voices including your own. In 2 Corinthians 11:14, it says, *"For Satan himself transforms himself into an angel of light"* to deceive the children of God. So many believers are imprisoned by their thoughts, thinking that every word that comes to their mind is from God. The devil is crafty, and if we are not careful, he can lead us the wrong path and destroy our lives. First John 4:1 says, *"Beloved, do not believe every spirit, but test the spirits to see whether they are from God..."* Throughout my Christian walk, I continue to diligently seek the assistance of the Holy Spirit to help me discern the voice of God and improve my hearing in the spirit realm.

I have been asked, "How do you know God speaks? Does God still speak to us today?" First and foremost, I know God speaks because He has spoken to me so many times. Also, throughout the Bible God spoke to his children. God is still God. He has never changed and will never change. Hebrews 13:8 says,

"Jesus Christ the same yesterday, today and forever." Yes, God still speaks today.

John 8:47 says if you are of God, you will hear Him, but if you are not of God, you cannot hear Him. It is imperative we stay connected to God if we are to hear Him clearly. I know a lot of unbelievers and Christians who do not think God speaks. God speaks all the time, and He wants to talk to us, but we often just do not have time for Him. Why do some of us not hear from God? Living in sin can be a hindrance from hearing from God. A poor relationship with Him, ignorance, and pride can also be a barrier to hearing from God.

Sometimes we are so full of ourselves. We may think we have got the whole world in *our* hands. So, who is God to tell us what to do or how to live our lives? Then, the moment we find ourselves in trouble we are calling on God for help. How on earth did we think we could live life without God? He created humans in His own image and likeness, and we are His children. Children are never greater or bigger than their parents. We are not bigger than God our Creator. John 10:27 says, *"My sheep hear my voice, and I know them, and they follow me."* When God is your Shepherd and you are His sheep, you will hear His voice and follow Him.

How does God speak to us? Here are some ways that God has spoken to me. I believe He can speak to you too if you are willing to hear from Him.

THROUGH THE SCRIPTURES

Have you ever encountered God speaking to you as you read your Bible? Sometimes certain words may jump at you or grab hold of your heart or attention. That is God trying to speak to you. Some of us may want to hear a loud voice when God may not want to do that just yet. So, be alert and be open to however God wants to speak to you. In my walk with God, He continues to use the Scriptures to speak to me. His words corrected me and instructed me to address my unpleasant attitude and behaviors. He gave me directions on how to handle difficult situations in my life. I encourage you to pick up the Bible and read it. If you do not know where to start, start with the New Testament because it is filled with Jesus' teachings. I believe God will speak to you when you dive into His word.

THE PREACHED WORD OF GOD

Romans 10:14-15 says, *"How then shall they call on Him in whom they have not believed? And how shall they believe in Him whom they have not heard? And shall they hear without a preacher?"* God used sermons to speak to me. As a preacher begins to divide the word, the Holy Spirit knowing the hearts and conditions of everyone, takes the word and specifically tailors it to address each person's situation. This is powerful and awesome! Only God can do this!

There was this time when a preacher came to my church program, and I was going through a tough time in my marriage. I was sitting there feeling broken and defeated with no hope in sight. As the preacher began to preach, he began to give a testimony of his own past troubled marriage and how God restored his family. Then he said something about trusting God, and immediately, I heard God say to me, "Trust me!" I responded, "I trust you Lord!" But, I said it in a tune of "What do you mean trust me?" Then, the Spirit of the Lord said it again and added, "Trust me COMPLETELY!" The moment I heard the word completely, I understood what God meant. I gave Him some areas of my life while holding back on others. If we are to trust God, we must trust Him completely and not hold back anything.

IMPRESSION IN YOUR HEART

Sometimes from nowhere, you get an impression in your heart about something you have never thought about, and suddenly you have this download of information. An impression is something that grabs your attention and pulls you. It is so strong that God brings your full attention to it. Sometimes, you try to water it down, and it does not go away. It is important to cross check the impression against the word of God to make sure it aligns with the word of God. Do not jump into anything. Pray and fast for clarity.

PRAYER AND FASTING

Through my life experiences, I found out you can hear from God through fasting and praying. Fasting is a powerful spiritual discipline that deepens our relationship with God and promotes our ability to clearly hear from Him. Fasting from food with intentional prayers helps us to stay focused and deepen our communion with God, making it easier to hear His voice. Fasting eradicates physical distractions and ushers us into the presence of God. It was through my difficult life challenges that I seriously took on fasting and praying, which brought me to a place of humility and dependence. It allowed me to hold on to His words. The more I sought Him, the closer I became to Him. My spiritual senses increased, and it made it easier for me to hear from Him and follow His directions.

Before you start fasting, determine why you are doing it. Are you seeking God's face for guidance, a spiritual breakthrough, or to draw closer to Him? After that, prepare your spirit by reading Scriptures and be attentive to every word. Ask God to help you hear His voice. If you are new to fasting, start small. You can fast from one meal a day and gradually extend your fast as the spirit of God leads you. Fasting and praying is a profound way to position ourselves to hear from God, allowing us to step away from the noise of daily life and focus on His voice.

AUDIBLE VOICE

I think this is the most fascinating one to me. I never knew God could speak audibly until it happened to me. This is when you hear Him audibly just like you hear other people speaking. But, His voice is distinct from every other voice. It is calm, peaceful, reassuring, and loving. At first, it seemed weird to me. Why am I hearing this voice? As you continue to develop your relationship with God, the voice becomes clearer and recognizable. John 10:27-28 says, *"My sheep hear my voice and I know them, and they follow me."* As you dine with God daily, his voice becomes part of you.

A long time ago, hearing the audible voice of God saved my life. I was 24 years old and started Hudson Valley Community college for my associate degree in nursing. I was running late to class, so I took a side road by the classroom building close to the parking lot. The road was narrow, about the size of one and half parking spaces. This particular road had a blind spot between the building and the parking lot, so if students were coming out of the building to the parking lot, they would not be able to see a car coming and neither would the driver be able to see a student coming out of the building. So, I was driving from the direction of this blind spot at a high speed. Suddenly, I heard a loud voice say,

"STOP!" There was no time to think or ask the LORD any questions because the voice sounded so urgent. I obeyed the voice immediately. I slammed my legs on my brakes and my car shook vigorously and came to a stop.

When I lifted up my head, a student was in front of my car. My entire body began to quiver, and the student looked surprised, perhaps wondering how on earth did I know to stop the car? I later found out that cars are only to exit the school building from that side road. Hearing the voice of God saved me from killing that student. Could you imagine the impact that would have had on my life?

INNER VOICE

There is more than one inner voice - the voice of the Holy Spirit, your mind (your thoughts, intents and actions), and the voice of your spirit man, which communicates with your flesh and is in constant battle with good and evil. The most important voice for us to recognize is the voice of the Holy Spirit because it will bring us comfort and security. The Holy Spirit communicates with our spirit man (Spirit to spirit). It is important for you to familiarize yourself with the voices that speak to you, whether they are of your mind, the devil, or of God. This is where most of us get messed up. The majority of the time our mind (logical thoughts) speaks volume and sometimes with unclear facts and reasoning. Although some of our thoughts may seem reasonable, they could be far from the truth. We need the help of the Holy Spirit to empower and quicken our spirit man to bring things under His submission for clarity. The battle of our mind can be defeated by the Holy Spirit who has the utmost power to conquer and quench all fiery darts of our thoughts. But, we must allow and give the Holy Spirit permission to speak to our situation and problems. When you stay connected to God, you get to hear the Holy Spirit's directions. He becomes the master of your entire life. He does not want half of you, though. He wants you completely to Himself. Are you willing to surrender yourself to Him?

DREAMS

I read an article in Medical News Today titled, "What Does It Mean When We Dream?" By Hannah Nichols. In this article, dream is defined as *a universal human experience that can be described as a state of consciousness characterized by sensory, cognitive and emotional occurrences during sleep.* She explained the five phases of sleep in a sleep cycle. Dreams most likely happen during deep sleep, also known as REM sleep. Hannah says this stage accounts for 20-25 percent of total sleep time. Every one of us dreams, however, some of us may not remember our dreams. But, that does not mean we do not dream. Hannah also pointed out that *dreams are stories and images our minds create while we sleep. They can be entertaining, fun, romantic, disturbing, frightening, and sometimes bizarre. Our dreams can represent our unconscious desires and wishes.* That means, sometimes what we think about during the day may appear in our dreams. It is important to identify which of our dreams comes from our conscious or unconscious minds and which ones are direct messages from God. Pray to God for discernment.

God speaks through dreams. In the Bible, God gave Joseph a glimpse of his future through multiple dreams that came to fruition. Genesis 37 narrates Joseph's dreams and how he shared them with his brothers. In one of the dreams he stated, *"We were binding sheaves of grain out in the field when suddenly my sheaf rose and stood upright, while your sheaves gathered around mine and bowed down to it."* Joseph's dream came to pass when he became the second chief-in-command in Egypt. During the famine across the land, Joseph's brothers, who sold him to the Midianites, came and bowed down to Joseph because they were in search of food for their family. God still speaks to us through our dreams today. In my life, God had given me many dreams about others and myself that have come to pass in real life. One day, I was praying for a very good friend of mine for the fruit of the womb. I spent a lot of time in the presence of God seeking God's divine blessing for this sister. One day I had a vivid dream. My friend had a baby girl, and we went to her house to celebrate this gift of life from God. We were at this huge house and I was standing at the back of a beckon looking into the family room and the kitchen. The dream was so vivid and felt so real. But, it was a dream! After a year or so, not only did my friend buy a large house, she had a baby girl as well! Yes, God speaks through dreams!

VISIONS

God has revealed so many secret things to me through visions. Things that would have never crossed my mind. Yes, God can speak to us through visions. Proverbs 29:19 says, *"Where there is no vision, the people perish…."* In Habakkuk 2:3 *it says, "The vision is for an appointed time, that although it may tarry, we should wait for it because it will come to fruition."* I love how God reveals His secrets to His children. When I went back to school for my bachelor's degree in nursing, I wanted to become a nurse manager. But less than a month after I graduated with my Bachelor of Science in Nursing, God instructed me to become a nurse practitioner so that I could help more people. I really did not want to go back to school. I asked God to prove it if that was Him speaking to me. Frankly, I knew it was God without a doubt, but I wanted an excuse not to do it.

A few days later I had a vision where it seemed like I was watching a television or motion picture of myself. I had a long white coat on with my stethoscope around my neck and a nursing cap on my head. I saw myself assessing a patient's heart who was lying in a hospital bed. After this revelation, I knew God truly wanted me to become a nurse practitioner. So, I obeyed the LORD and went back to school part time. Three years later, I graduated with my master's degree as a family nurse practitioner. Today, I work in a hospital taking care of patients. It is vital to test all spirits to determine whether they are of God. God is sovereign and powerful. He knows everything about us, and He is willing to reveal Himself to us. To start the process of hearing from God, we need to stay connected to Him to develop a close relationship. The closer you are to Him, the better the flow of His words and His presence.

Chapter 7

HOW CAN I FORGET?

I grew up in a small community in Benin City, Edo State, Nigeria. As I reflect on my earlier years of childhood, I can recall many exciting moments, as well as difficult times. Yes, Nigeria has its own political and economic challenges like other countries, but that did not take away the good times I had as a child with my family and friends. Family ties were always the core of my upbringing. It was where I found encouragement, strength, correction, togetherness and love. I came from a large family. I am the fourth of nine children.

I was not born with a silver spoon. My family was middle-class, although there was a time when my parents had some financial challenges. My dad is an educated, ex-police officer, and my mom was a stay-at-home mom with no education. Yet, she was brilliant! She was gifted with great wisdom that empowered her to thrive, not only as a business woman, but as someone who was great at building relationships with people. Mom once told me there was a time when many parents did not see the need and value to educate young girls because they felt a woman's duty was to meet her husband's sexual desires, have kids, cook, and keep the house. So, sending girls to school was a waste of their financial investment. What a terrible mindset? Thankfully, this thinking has shifted. Today, more girls are educated and are making great contributions to their society like never before.

In my teenage years, Mom shared an incredible event that happened when I was two months old. She said my older siblings had gone to school and Dad was at work when she left me in bed to make some food in the kitchen. When she returned to check on me, she found me lifeless. She picked me up and began to scream for help. The neighbors came, but no one could help. Unlike in the United States where you can call 911 for help, there was no emergency line to call. She said, "I cried out to God for help in the middle of the chaos, and suddenly, life came into you." This story showed me how God has a special interest in me, and He is the master of my life, my shield, and my protector.

Growing up in my household, I had some responsibilities and contributions I had to make to keep the family running. Home chores, cooking, and overseeing my younger siblings were basic obligations for me and my older siblings. I also helped Mom with her small convenient store, and I did street hawking – selling drinks and snacks along the road. My siblings also had their specific duties to foster the family's well-being and survival. These experiences taught me strong family values, hard work, self-respect, confidence, resilience, and discipline, which contributed to my success in the United States. My

Dr. Tina Omorogbe

parents taught us the importance of family and the need to stay connected no matter what life threw at us.

At the age of 22, I had the opportunity to travel to the United States to continue my education. I joined my two older brothers who were here, before I later met my husband. My first few months in the United States were tough because it was my first time away from home. I felt isolated from friends and families. My older brothers were rarely home because they had to work. Several months after, I started my first job, and the feeling of isolation began to lift as I assimilated to my new environment and made new friends. A year and half later, I met my husband, and we later got married. We have been married for 34 years. We have three beautiful children and three awesome grandsons.

When I was in 7th grade, a group of nurses came to my school to administer vaccinations to protect us against communicable diseases. It was there where I fell in love with the nursing profession. Ever since, I dreamt of becoming a nurse because of my caring and compassionate spirit and love for people. So, after two years in the United States, I started my nursing education at a community college where I completed my associate degree in Applied Science in Nursing and became a registered nurse. I worked as a bedside nurse for nine years before I completed my online bachelor's degree in Science of

95

Nursing (BSN). It was not an easy journey working full time, caring for family, and attending school as a part-time student. But, this was my way of pursuing the *American dream*. The idea of obtaining the American dream motivated me to pursue my education to reach financial freedom and a better life for me and my family. But often, the American dream seemed harder to achieve than ever.

Finishing my BSN program was pretty exhausting and mentally draining. I was happy to be done and was looking forward to getting a job as a nurse manager. Then, I heard the unthinkable. I was getting ready for work one morning when the Spirit of the LORD spoke to me and said I should go back to school. I rebuked the voice, and I told Satan to get behind me! The LORD spoke the second time and said I will be able to help more people and treat their conditions. As much as I did not want to go back to school, deep down in my heart, I knew it was God speaking, and I had to obey Him. The rest was history. Two months after completing my BSN, I started a part-time program to get my master's degree in Nursing with a specialty in Family Health. Three years later, I graduated and passed my board certification as a family nurse practitioner. After practicing as a nurse practitioner for six years, I went back to school to obtain my terminal degree with a doctorate in Nursing Practice. As I reflect on my life's journey, I am in awe of what God has done in my life. Who would have thought, in my early years, I would amount to anything or accomplish what I have attained today? My journey through life's deep waters and valleys has profoundly catapulted me to a place of peace, humility, grace, and gratitude.

As life began to unfold in my new environment, I had so much on my plate as I pursued my American dream. My relationship with God began to weaken because I was not spending much time with Him like I used to in my teenage years in Nigeria. This is a place you never want to be. But if you find yourself in a place where God seems far away from you, I recommend you drop everything that is consuming your time at the feet of Jesus and surrender your life to Him completely and repent. His arms are wide open to receive you back. I found myself in this desolate and empty place. I felt lifeless and lonely. This was when I cried out to God for help.

God sometimes allows us to go through difficult and unpleasant things in life, but it is never His desire to leave us in a painful situation. He allowed the devil to take me for a little ride into the storm of life. I almost gave up everything and threw in the towel. I knew that was not the best thing for my family and me. So, I made a choice to trust God. Sometimes when you are going through difficult situations and friends and family abandon you, that is the best time to turn to God. I want you to know God sees you, and He is close to you. You are not alone. He is standing by you whether you know it or not. Do not put God in a human box. "He is watching me suffer," some may say. No, God does not take delight in our suffering. It makes Him sad when we do not bring our troubles to Him in the first place. God is always present, and He sees our pains. Deuteronomy 31:8 says, *"The Lord himself goes before you and will be with you; he will never leave you nor forsake you. Do not be afraid; do not be discouraged."*

In my darkest moments, every door I tried to escape through was shut against my face. I felt like God purposefully shut every door so I could face Him and not escape. It was time to stop running from God. In my brokenness and pain, God began to reveal myself to me, my purpose, and His divine calling for my life. I was disconnected from God for a long time without even realizing it. God had to allow the storms of life into my life to reset my walk with Him. Jeremiah 17:5 says, *"Cursed is the one who trusts in man, who draws strength from mere flesh and whose heart turns away from the Lord."* God wanted me to put my trust in Him completely, not in humans.

Sometimes when we are entangled with the issues of life, we often ask God to take the painful issue away. We question Him by saying, "LORD, why don't you take the pain away? Why did this and that happen? Why did you allow that person to abuse or betray me? Why did you neglect me?" Have you ever asked

God why? I have so many times. One morning as I was getting ready for work, I began to reflect on my past. Suddenly, heaviness and sadness overcame me. I started asking God why He was so silent when I was going through the tough times in my life. I did not expect an answer right away, but He answered and said, "I did it for your good." But wait a minute, how can anything good come out of pain? At the time, I did not understand it. But, now I recognize we have a God who takes painful situations and makes something good out of it. God is a good gift giver! He is always on time, and His timing is unbeatable. Are you struggling with the issues of life? Remember, it does not matter how you started, how you got there, or where you are right now. God wants to bring you out of that painful situation to a place of peace and joy.

So, how do I do that? I am glad you asked! First, take the matter from your hands and place it in God's hands. Stop overthinking your troubles. Instead, renew your mind with the word of God. God has an answer for every problem you may have. Seek God's face and spend time with Him by reading the Bible, and you will get the instructions and directions that you need to transform your life. Staying in your past drains your energy and leaves you empty and discouraged. I was able to get back on my feet after I developed a close relationship with God. A relationship without God is like a single rope that is easily broken. I am grateful for my troubles because they made me stronger and catapulted my faith to a higher level. Today, I am bold like a lioness because of what I have been through. I am thankful for God's unwavering love for me.

How can I forget, O LORD, the pain, shame, and insults you took for me on the cross of calvary to set me free from my sins? How can I forget when you saved my life from an undiagnosed illness in my teenage years? How can I forget when you became my friend and confidante in a desolate place? How can I forget how you stood by me when I was lonely? How can I forget when you took my ashes and soul wounds and gave me beauty and healing? How can I forget when you took my brokenness and bitterness and gave me your love, joy and peace? How can I forget when you gave me victory and blessings beyond my imaginations when my enemies tried to destroy me? How can I forget the wonderful and awesome things you have done for me? I stand to declare the greatness and mighty works of God in my life!

Psalm 103, reminds us to not forget the benefits, advantages and rewards we get from God.

As people of God, we have eternal life through Christ Jesus. We have forgiveness of our sins, healing, provision, hope, joy, peace, protection, and security. In fact, we have uncountable and unlimited blessings. Throughout my life's journey, I can truly attest that I know God as the All Mighty (El- Shaddai), my LORD and Master (Adonai), my banner (Jehovah Nissi), my Shepherd (Jehovah Raah), my healer (Jehovah Rapha), my provider (Jehovah Jireh) and my peace (Jehovah Shalom). I am nobody without Him.

Often, as humans we have the tendency to forget the good things that have happened in our lives. We are good at remembering the bad stuff, not the good stuff. In the same manner, we have forgotten the goodness of God in our lives. Sadly, some of us have forgotten God, and we treat Him as if He does not exist. We go about our business trying to achieve the whole world. But, when we encounter difficult challenges in our lives, we suddenly call out to God for help. If you were in God's shoes, how would that make you feel? Well, the way It makes you feel is exactly the way it makes God feel.

So many of us are distracted by our busy daily activities that we hardly have time for God. Some people are intentional about setting their daily schedules and activities, while others just go with the flow of the day with no concrete plans. We do what seems best to us. But, can we create some time for God in our busy schedule? Most of us have forgotten that we are sheep in need of a shepherd. We cannot do life without our Creator. And, if we try to do life without God, we return broken and empty. John 15:5 says, *"I am the vine, you are the branches. He who abides in Me, and I in him, bears much fruit: for without Me you can do nothing."* God has been there for me since birth. I try to surrender my life completely to God. So should you!

As you go through the deep waters of life, be assured God knows what you are going through, and He knows the way out of your troubles. You just have to trust in Him to see you through your problems. Do not delay! God is faithful. He will come to you, comfort you, and show you the way to peace. Psalm 139 illustrates that the Lord is always near us. He knows when we are in deep trouble, he knows our thoughts, our pains and shortcomings. He knows it all! Before you say a word, He knows what you are going to say. He protects us with His powerful arms even when we are far from Him. God sees you even when you hide in darkness because darkness is like light to Him. Nothing you do is hidden before God. His thoughts are far beyond our understanding. So, trust God as you go through your troubles, and He will turn your bitter tears and sorrows into joy as He did for me.

How can I forget the marvelous works of God in my life? One fateful evening, I was lying in my bed minding my business when God instructed me to help people in the community by educating them about high blood pressure and screening them for the disease. At the time, I was not sure why God was so concerned about that, but I obeyed. I actually found out that millions of people were dying all over the world from this disease.

Years later, Chasing Health Inc. was born. I started Chasing Health as a nonprofit organization that renders hypertension education and blood pressure screenings to mostly people in underserved communities both locally and abroad. The organization has brought several hypertension initiatives on blood pressure prevention and management programs to Edo State, Nigeria. In January 2020, we had a successful hypertension campaign where we supplied multiple hypertension medications to hundreds of villagers in a local community. The women danced and praised God for hearing their prayers. I was happy to see their faces light up with joy. Chasing Health Inc. continues to impact local community health and wellbeing through collaboration with local organizations. Years later, Chasing Health Inc. launched Chasing Health Integrative Care to further provide more medical services.

I am a very spiritual person. I love God and I want to please Him. I fell in love with God when I was 17 years old. I was called by God to preach the good news of Jesus Christ. The only one true Savior of the world. One day, I had a vision where God took my right hand and anointed it with oil and blessed it, and suddenly, I saw fire go through my hand. After that experience, God began instructing me to pray with people. They were healed after I prayed. Sometimes, I feel like my right hand is on fire. I know God has given me His grace and love to impact people's lives, not only physically, but spiritually as well. I am greatly humbled and blessed to serve alongside the Holy Spirit, the one who does all the cleansing and healing.

Years later, I started the Hand of God Global Ministry. The organization is a nonprofit that seeks to share the love of God and the gospel of Jesus Christ through healing encounters for those who are physically and spiritually ill and broken. The premise of my calling is based on Isaiah 61:1 which says, *"The Spirit of the Lord God is upon me; because the Lord hath anointed me to preach good tidings unto the meek; he hath sent me to bind up the brokenhearted, to proclaim liberty to the captives and the opening of the prison to them that are bound."* Who but God would have thought I would have amounted to anything? I never believed I had anything to offer. I never believed in myself, but the God who knows and sees beyond what we see - and knows everything about me - believed in me. How can I ever forget His marvelous deeds?

Years back, God said He was going to do something new in my life, but I never perceived it would be to this extent. Sometimes, it is hard to believe in yourself when people around you tell you that you will never measure up or you are not good enough. It is difficult to dream big when the voices in your head are constantly reminding you why you cannot do anything substantial in your life. After all, you do not have anything to say or offer. And by the way, who cares about what you have to say? The list goes on and on. This is the battle of the mind, and we must take our thoughts back from the evil one. All you need to do is speak positive words of affirmation to yourself to negate the negative voices, believe in yourself, and stay focused. Tell the devil to SHUT UP! When I finally gave myself permission to take a leap of faith and trust God, I began to see positive growth and make strides to become the best version of myself. I continue to rise and soar by His grace and love for me.

How can I forget your marvelous works, O Lord? Psalm 103:2 -5 says, *"Praise the lord, O my soul, and forget not all his benefits, who forgives all my iniquity, who heals all my diseases, who redeems your life from the pit, who crowns you with steadfast love and mercy, who satisfies you with good so that your youth is renewed like the eagle's."* When I think of the goodness of God in my life, it feels so unreal because I know where He has brought me from and what He took me through to get to where I am today.

All my accomplishments were through God's revelations, direction and encouragement. It was through my tribulations and dark moments that I got closer to God. God taught me what it means to walk with Him. He taught me to love myself and others. He taught me how to forgive people who have hurt me so He could bless me. He taught me to be more intentional about my spiritual walk and to be present with Him by staying connected always and not sometimes. He taught me to be humble and to develop my listening skills. He taught me to trust Him COMPLETELY and to never lose my faith. He taught me to always keep my eye on Him.

I pray the content of this book helps you to locate God and fall in love with Him. I dare you to humble yourself before God, and follow His directions. He knows what is best for you and your family. There is no time to waste. Do it now. Say this prayer: *Heavenly Father, you are the God of the universe. You made me in your image and likeness because of the love you have for me. I thank you for this. I have sinned and gone astray from you. Please forgive me and accept me back through the death of your son Jesus Christ. Show me your love and grace. Teach me to follow you. Help me to hear you and never to depart from you again, in Jesus' name. Amen. Thank you God for accepting me into your kingdom.*

ACKNOWLEDGMENTS

I would like to thank my husband - Amen - and my three wonderful children - Uwa, Uyi and Nosa - for their unfailing love and encouragement through this journey. I am most grateful to my youngest daughter, Nosa, who is my tech guru and greatest supporter. I could not have done it without you, Nosa! I thank my family and friends for all their support through my spiritual journey and for allowing me to minister to them. I thank the Holy Spirit for believing in me when I did not believe in myself. I also acknowledge my three awesome grandchildren - Maverick, Makai and Marcell. They are my precious gifts from God. My heart is filled with so much joy. To God be all the glory!

ABOUT THE AUTHOR

DR. TINA OMOROGBE, DNP, MS, FNP-BC

Dr. Tina Omorogbe was born and raised in Nigeria, West Africa. She came to the United States in the late 1980s. She is married with three lovely children and three grandsons. She currently works in a hospital as a nurse practitioner. She has a doctorate degree in Nursing Practice.

With over 30 years of nursing experience, Dr. Omorogbe's clinical knowledge, expertise and love for people moved her to create Chasing Health Inc., an organization that provides health education and blood pressure screening to people in underserved communities locally and in Nigeria. Due to her passion to impact change, she started her private practice "Chasing Health Integrative Care" to further provide health equity and reduce health care disparity. Because of the impact of her work, she was featured on Channel 13 News Heart Beat with Benita Zahn to promote awareness and prevention of hypertension, stroke and cardiovascular disease.

Dr. Omorogbe is also the founder of the Hand of God Global Ministry, a nonprofit religious organization that brings healing, restoration and deliverance to people who are broken and in spiritual bondage. She holds a yearly healing conference that helps men and women experience not only the presence of God, but gain spiritual and physical healing. Dr Omorogbe was called and anointed by God to preach the gospel of Jesus Christ. She is a lover of God and a worshiper.

Dr. Omorogbe is the first elected female president of the Association of Nigerians in the Capital District, a cultural organization that promotes unity and strength among the Nigerians in her local community.

Dr. Omorogbe is an author, healthcare expert, and a motivational speaker. Her dream is to continue to impact the lives of people through the services she provides to people in her local community and abroad.

Milton Keynes UK
Ingram Content Group UK Ltd.
UKHW020917291124
451807UK00013B/973